June 2012

IRS 2013 BUDGET

Continuing to Improve Information on Program Costs and Results Could Aid in Resource Decision Making

GAO

Accountability ★ Integrity ★ Reliability

GAO-12-603

Contents

Figures

Abbreviations

ACA	Affordable Care Act
AMS	Account Management Services
AUR	Automated Underreporter Program
BSM	Business Systems Modernization
CADE	Customer Account Data Engine
CFO	Chief Financial Officer
CI	Criminal Investigation
CIO	Chief Information Officer
e-SVS	e-Services
EFDS	Electronic Fraud Detection System
EPO	Estimation Program Office
EUSS	IRS End User Systems and Services
EVM	earned value management
FATCA	Foreign Account Tax Compliance Act

FTE	full-time equivalent
HHS	Department of Health and Human Services
HIRIF	Health Insurance Reform Implementation Fund
HITCA	Health Insurance Tax Credit Administration
IMF	Individual Master File
ICCE	Integrated Customer Communication Environment
IDRS	Integrated Data Retrieval System
IFS	Integrated Financial System
IRDM	Information Reporting and Document Matching
IRS	Internal Revenue Service
ISRP	Integrated Submission and Remittance Processing
IT	information technology
MeF	Modernized e-File
MISSTU	Modernized Infrastructure Solaris 10 & Supporting Technologies Upgrade
MITS	Modernization and Information Technology Services
MSSS	IRS Main Frames and Servers Services and Support
OMB	Office of Management and Budget
PPACA	Patient Protection and Affordable Care Act
ROI	return on investment
RRP	Return Review Program
SAN	Storage Area Network
SCRIPS	Service Center Recognition/Image Processing System
Treasury	Department of the Treasury
TSS	IRS Telecommunications Systems and Support
WBS	work breakdown structure

G A O
Accountability * Integrity * Reliability

United States Government Accountability Office
Washington, DC 20548

June 8, 2012

The Honorable Richard J. Durbin
Chairman
The Honorable Jerry Moran
Ranking Member
Subcommittee on Financial Services and General Government
Committee on Appropriations
United States Senate

The Honorable Charles W. Boustany, Jr.
Chairman
The Honorable John Lewis
Ranking Member
Subcommittee on Oversight
Committee on Ways and Means
United States House of Representatives

This letter transmits several briefings we provided between February 27, 2012 and May 16, 2012, as well as subsequent comments from the Internal Revenue Service (IRS). See appendix I for the final, updated briefing.

The President requested $12.8 billion for IRS for fiscal year 2013. This is an 8 percent increase over the enacted appropriation for fiscal year 2012, and follows a 2.5 percent decrease between fiscal year 2011 and fiscal year 2012. Because of the size of IRS's budget and the importance of its service and compliance programs for all taxpayers, you asked us to review the fiscal year 2013 budget justification for IRS as well as how it absorbed the prior year's reductions. Based on discussions with your offices, our objectives were to: (1) describe how IRS managed funding reductions in fiscal year 2012; (2) describe the fiscal year 2013 budget request for IRS and budget and staffing trends from fiscal year 2009 through fiscal year 2013; (3) evaluate any new enforcement and infrastructure initiatives in the fiscal year 2013 budget request, including whether return on investment (ROI) estimates are provided; (4) evaluate the reliability of IRS's cost estimate for implementing its responsibilities under the Patient Protection and Affordable Care Act (PPACA);[1] (5) evaluate the amount requested for hiring additional staff in fiscal year 2013; (6) evaluate the performance of IRS's major information technology (IT) investments; (7) list any analyses we have done related to legislative proposals included in the budget request for IRS; and (8) describe IRS's progress implementing our prior budget presentation recommendations and list our open matters for Congress and recommendations to IRS regarding tax administration with potential budget savings or revenue increases.

To conduct this work, we addressed the first three objectives by reviewing IRS's plans to manage budget reductions and examining trends in selected performance measures since 2007, identifying prior GAO work that could increase efficiencies, and comparing and analyzing budget documentation from fiscal year 2008 through fiscal year 2013. We compared the reliability of the PPACA cost estimate with best practices outlined in the GAO *Cost Estimating and Assessment Guide*[2] (*Cost Guide*) using documents, such as work breakdown structures (WBS), and interviewing IRS PPACA officials. We reviewed cost estimates for PPACA implementation based on your interest and because it represented the largest requested increase in the budget proposal. To evaluate the amount requested for hiring additional staff in fiscal year 2013, we compared Office of Management and Budget (OMB) *Circular A-11* guidance with IRS's budgeting practices for funding the hiring of new staff. We reviewed IRS's recent hiring patterns and calculated the percentage of staff hired in each quarter for new initiatives in fiscal year 2009 and fiscal year 2010. We used a $100,000/full-time equivalent (FTE)[3] value for salary and benefits, which IRS officials told us they commonly use as an approximate cost per FTE, and compared it with the budget request to determine differences. We reviewed reported cost and

---

[1]IRS is one of several agencies charged with implementing PPACA, legislation aimed at reforming the private insurance market and expanding health coverage to the uninsured. IRS is responsible for implementing PPACA provisions relating to, among other things, new taxes, tax credits, and information reporting requirements. Pub. L. No. 111-148, 124 Stat.119 (March 23, 2010), as amended by the Health Care and Education Reconciliation Act of 2010, Pub. L. No. 111-152, 124 Stat. 1029 (Mar. 30, 2010).

[2]GAO, *Cost Estimating and Assessment Guide: Best Practices for Developing and Managing Capital Program Costs*, GAO-09-3SP (Washington, D.C.: Mar. 2, 2009).

[3]A FTE is a measure of staff hours equal to those of an employee who works 2,080 hours per year, or 40 hours per week for 52 weeks.

schedule information and Chief Information Officer (CIO) assessments for all IRS major IT investments and interviewed officials in the Modernization and Information Technology Services (MITS) office. We also reviewed legislative proposals in the budget justification and identified prior, related GAO work. Finally, we obtained information on prior-year budget recommendations from various IRS officials and reviewed relevant documentation, including the fiscal year 2013 Congressional Budget Justification, to determine which recommendations were implemented and we relied on prior work and examined open matters and recommendations with a potential to increase savings or revenues. For each objective, we interviewed IRS officials in the offices of the Chief Financial Officer (CFO) and Corporate Budgeting. We conducted our work in Washington, D.C., where key IRS officials involved with the budget and IT systems are located.

We conducted this performance audit from November 2011 to June 2012 in accordance with generally accepted government auditing standards. Those standards require that we plan and perform the audit to obtain sufficient, appropriate evidence to provide a reasonable basis for our findings and conclusions based on our audit objectives. We believe that the evidence obtained provides a reasonable basis for our findings and conclusions based on our audit objectives. We spoke with IRS officials and reviewed data collection procedures and determined that the data used in this report were sufficiently reliable for our purposes.

The results of our work show:

- IRS absorbed the 2.5 percent or $305 million fiscal year 2012 reduction by decreasing FTEs and other costs, primarily in the Enforcement and Operations Support appropriations. Several of our recent reports show that other opportunities exist to increase efficiencies through, for example, automating some services, leveraging paid tax return preparers, and conducting more compliance checks before issuing refunds.
- IRS's fiscal year 2013 budget request represents a $944.5 million (8.0 percent) and about a 4,500 FTEs (5.0 percent) increase over fiscal year 2012.
- Seven of the 12 proposed new program initiatives ($603.1 million) are supported by ROI estimates; the others ($303.9 million) are not supported by ROI information or, for the 2 we reviewed, other similar economic assessments, such as cost effectiveness analyses.
- IRS's PPACA cost estimate partially meets best practices for reliability, but it has not been updated since October 2010.

- IRS budgets for hiring new staff based on the new staff being on-board for the full fiscal year. But, in recent years, IRS hired most new staff late in the fiscal year, which could have resulted in funding being used for other purposes that are not described or substantiated in the budget justification.
- Fourteen of 20 major IT investments were within 10 percent of cost and schedule estimates between October 2011 and March 2012, but we could not determine whether these investments delivered planned functionality because IRS does not have a quantitative measure of scope for major IT investments.
- We have conducted analyses related to 6 of the 22 legislative proposals included in the budget request for IRS.
- IRS at least partially implemented 5 of our 9 prior recommendations intended to improve information presented in the budget request; in addition, we have 106 other matters for Congress or recommendations to IRS regarding tax administration that remain open and could result in potential financial benefits, either budget savings or increases in tax revenue.

Conclusions

We have identified several areas where budget decision makers lack information that would be helpful in making decisions about resource trade-offs at IRS.

- Unlike most enforcement initiatives that IRS now justifies with ROI estimates, non-enforcement investment initiatives are not justified with similar economic analyses, such as cost-effectiveness analyses. When comparisons of alternative investments for accomplishing a goal do not consider costs, budget decision makers cannot be assured that alternatives were fully evaluated and that the best alternative was selected.
- Without a timely, updated cost estimate for PPACA, budget decision makers will not know the fraction of the multi-year effort being funded in fiscal year 2013 or the subsequent remaining costs.
- Because the budget request for hiring new staff is not based on expected hiring dates, but instead assumes hiring will occur at the beginning of the fiscal year, some funds will be available for other uses, which are not described or substantiated in the budget request.
- Although IRS tracks the schedule and cost performance of IT investments, it does not have a quantitative measure to determine whether it is delivering planned functionality. Without this measure, budget decision makers lack complete information about IRS's performance in managing IT investment projects.

Recommendations for Executive Action

To continue to improve information on program cost and results that could aid in resource decision making, we recommend that the Commissioner of Internal Revenue

- ensure cost-effectiveness analyses are conducted for future significant investments when there are alternative approaches for achieving a given benefit, such as for any new significant PPACA projects;
- ensure that an updated PPACA cost estimate is completed by September 2012 in accordance with best practices in the GAO *Cost Guide;*
- prepare funding requests for new staff based on estimated hiring dates; and
- develop a quantitative measure of scope, at a minimum for its major IT investments, to have complete information on the performance of these investments.

Agency Comments and Our Evaluation

We provided a draft of this report to the Commissioner of Internal Revenue for his review and comment. The CFO provided written comments as an email attachment, which is reprinted in appendix II. IRS also provided us with technical comments, which we incorporated into the report as appropriate.

In response to our draft report, the CFO stated that IRS agreed with three of our four recommendations.

- For the two recommendations regarding PPACA, IRS agreed with them, but stated our report did not acknowledge that the majority of the funding is to support ongoing efforts and for staff already on board in fiscal year 2012. On the contrary, our report describes in detail (in the background, in the section on fiscal year 2012 funding reductions, and in the section on fiscal year 2013 budget data and trends) the funding IRS received from the Health Insurance Reform Implementation Fund in fiscal years 2010, 2011 and 2012, including FTEs funded in prior years.

- IRS agreed with our recommendation to develop a quantitative measure of scope, but the CFO stated that IRS has other methods in place to document delivered functionality of a project throughout the life-cycle. We agree that the methods identified address project functionality, but they do not provide a quantitative measure of performance.

- IRS did not agree with our recommendation to prepare funding requests for new staff based on estimated hiring dates. The CFO stated that IRS is committed to transparency in spending though the submission of the annual Operating Plan and requests to reprogram funds as a result of the late enactment of the budget or delayed hiring of new staff. Our report emphasizes transparency in the budget request and discusses the issues raised in the CFO's letter. Transparency in the budget request is critical for Congressional oversight and decision making. IRS's current approach for budgeting for hiring new staff could result in substantial funding—about $300 million in fiscal year 2013— that could be used for other purposes that are not substantiated or described in the budget justification. We therefore believe our recommendation remains valid.

We plan to send copies of this report to the Chairman and Ranking Members of other Senate and House committees and subcommittees that have appropriation, authorization, and oversight responsibilities for IRS. We are also sending copies to the Commissioner of Internal Revenue, the Secretary of the Treasury, the Chairman of the IRS Oversight Board, and the Director of the Office of Management and Budget. Copies are also available at no charge on the GAO web site at http://www.gao.gov.

If you or your staffs have any questions or wish to discuss the material in this report further, please contact me at (202) 512-9110 or whitej@gao.gov. Contact points for our offices of Congressional Relations and Public Affairs may be found on the last page of this report. GAO staff members who made major contributions to this report are listed in appendix VII.

James R. White
Director, Tax Issues
Strategic Issues

Appendix I: Briefing Slides

IRS 2013 Budget: Continuing to Improve Information on Program Costs and Results Could Aid in Resource Decision Making

Prepared for the Subcommittee on Financial Services and General Government, Committee on Appropriations, U.S. Senate (May 15, 2012)
and the
Subcommittee on Oversight, Committee on Ways and Means, U.S. House of Representatives (May 16, 2012)
Updated (June 6, 2012)

Introduction

- The President requested $12.8 billion for the Internal Revenue Service (IRS) for fiscal year 2013. This is an 8 percent increase over the enacted appropriation for fiscal year 2012, and follows a 2.5 percent decrease between fiscal year 2011 and fiscal year 2012.

- Because of the size of IRS's budget and the importance of its service and compliance programs for all taxpayers, you asked us to review the fiscal year 2013 budget justification for IRS as well as how it absorbed fiscal year 2012 reductions. Other special areas of interest include an evaluation of the cost estimates for the Patient Protection and Affordable Care Act (PPACA)[1] initiatives and budgeting practices for funding the hiring of new staff.

[1] IRS is one of several agencies charged with implementing PPACA, legislation aimed at reforming the private insurance market and expanding health coverage to the uninsured. IRS is responsible for implementing PPACA provisions relating to, among other things, new taxes, tax credits, and information reporting requirements. Pub. L. No. 111-148, 124 Stat.119 (Mar. 23, 2010), as amended by the Health Care and Education Reconciliation Act of 2010, Pub. L. No. 111-152, 124 Stat. 1029 (Mar. 30, 2010).

Page 2

Objectives

Based on your request, our objectives were to:

(1) describe how IRS managed funding reductions in fiscal year 2012;

(2) describe the fiscal year 2013 budget request for IRS and budget and staffing trends from fiscal year 2009 through fiscal year 2013;

(3) evaluate any new enforcement and infrastructure initiatives in the fiscal year 2013 budget request, including whether return on investment (ROI) estimates are provided;

(4) evaluate the reliability of IRS's cost estimate for implementing its responsibilities under the PPACA;

(5) evaluate the amount requested for hiring additional staff in fiscal year 2013;

(6) evaluate the performance of IRS's major information technology (IT) investments;

(7) list any analyses we have done related to legislative proposals included in the budget request for IRS; and

(8) describe IRS's progress implementing our prior budget presentation recommendations and list our open matters for Congress and recommendations to IRS regarding tax administration with potential budget savings or revenue increases.

Page 3

Scope and Methodology

- To conduct our review, we
  - addressed the first three objectives by reviewing IRS's plans to manage budget reductions and examining trends in selected performance measures since 2007; identifying prior GAO work that could increase efficiencies; and comparing and analyzing budget documentation from fiscal year 2008 through fiscal year 2013;
  - compared the reliability of the cost estimates for PPACA with best practices outlined in the GAO *Cost Guide*[1] using documents, such as work breakdown structures, and interviewing IRS PPACA officials; we reviewed cost estimates for PPACA implementation based on your interest and because it represented the largest requested increase in the budget request;
  - compared Office of Management and Budget (OMB) *Circular A-11* guidance with IRS's budgeting practices for funding the hiring of new staff; reviewed recent hiring patterns and calculated the percent of staff hired in each quarter for new initiatives in fiscal year 2009 and fiscal year 2010; we used a $100,000/full-time equivalent[2] (FTE) value for salary and benefits, which IRS officials told us they commonly use as an approximate cost per FTE, and compared with the budget request to determine differences;
  - reviewed reported cost and schedule information and Department of the Treasury (Treasury) Chief Information Officer (CIO) assessments for all IRS major IT systems and interviewed officials in the Modernization and Information Technology Services (MITS) office;[3]

[1] See GAO, *Cost Estimating and Assessment Guide: Best Practices for Developing and Managing Capital Program Costs*, GAO-09-3SP (Washington, D.C.: Mar. 2, 2009).

[2] A FTE is a measure of staff hours equal to those of an employee who works 2,080 hours per year, or 40 hours per week for 52 weeks.
[3] Among other IT responsibilities, MITS has primary responsibility for managing and delivering IRS's Business Systems Modernization program.

Page 4

Scope and Methodology (continued)

- reviewed legislative proposals in the fiscal year 2013 Congressional Budget Justification and identified our prior related work; and
- obtained information on the status of prior year budget recommendations from various IRS officials and reviewed documentation, including the fiscal year 2013 Congressional Budget Justification, to determine which recommendations were implemented; and we relied on prior work and examined open matters and recommendations with a potential to increase savings or revenues.

- For each objective we interviewed officials in the IRS offices of Chief Financial Officer (CFO) and Corporate Budgeting. We conducted our work in Washington, D.C., where key IRS officials involved with the budget and IT systems are located.
- We conducted this performance audit from November 2011 to June 2012 in accordance with generally accepted government auditing standards. Those standards require that we plan and perform the audit to obtain sufficient, appropriate evidence to provide a reasonable basis for our findings and conclusions based on our audit objectives. We believe that the evidence obtained provides a reasonable basis for our findings and conclusions based on our audit objectives. We spoke with IRS officials and reviewed data collection procedures and determined that the data presented in this report were sufficiently reliable for our purposes.

Page 5

Results in Brief

- IRS absorbed the 2.5 percent or $305 million fiscal year 2012 reduction by decreasing FTEs and other costs, primarily in the Enforcement and Operations Support appropriations, but opportunities to increase efficiencies and more strategically manage operations exist.
- IRS's fiscal year 2013 budget request represents a $944.5 million (8.0 percent) and about a 4,500 FTE (5.0 percent) increase over fiscal year 2012.
- Seven of the 12 proposed new program initiatives ($603.1 million) are supported by ROI estimates; the others ($303.9 million) are not supported by ROI information or, for the 2 we reviewed, other similar economic assessments, such as cost-effectiveness analyses.
- IRS's PPACA cost estimate partially meets best practices for reliability, but it has not been updated since October 2010.
- IRS budgets for hiring new staff based on them being on-board for the full fiscal year. But, in recent years, it hired most new staff late in the fiscal year, which could have resulted in funding being used for other purposes that are not described or substantiated in the budget justification.
- Fourteen of 20 major IT investments were within 10 percent of cost and schedule estimates between October 2011 and March 2012, but we could not determine whether these investments delivered planned functionality because IRS does not have a quantitative measure of scope for major IT investments.
- We have conducted analyses related to 6 of the 22 legislative proposals included in the budget request for IRS.
- IRS at least partially implemented 5 of our 9 prior recommendations intended to improve information presented in the budget request; in addition, we have 106 other matters for Congress or recommendations to IRS regarding tax administration that remain open and could result in potential financial benefits, either budget savings or increases in tax revenue.

Page 6

Background

IRS's Budget Presentation

• IRS's budget presentation has three levels—appropriations, budget activities, and program activities.

• Requested funding increases for new program initiatives, such as implementing tax legislative changes, may be included within multiple appropriations or budget activities. The budget justification does not link new initiatives to program activities.

Figure 1: Three Levels of IRS's Budget Presentation

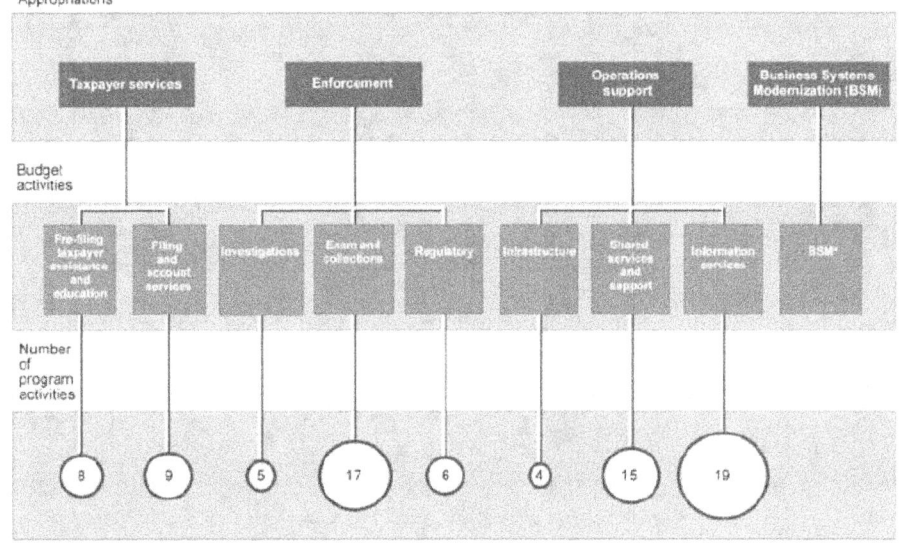

Source: Fiscal year 2013 Congressional Budget Justification for IRS.

ªThe BSM budget activity does not include any specific program activities.

Page 7

Background

Budget Process Timeline

• IRS's budget process begins about 18 months prior to the final submission and is guided by the IRS Commissioner, Deputy Commissioners, CFO, and Corporate Budget office.

Figure 2: Timeline of IRS's Fiscal Year 2013 Budget Process

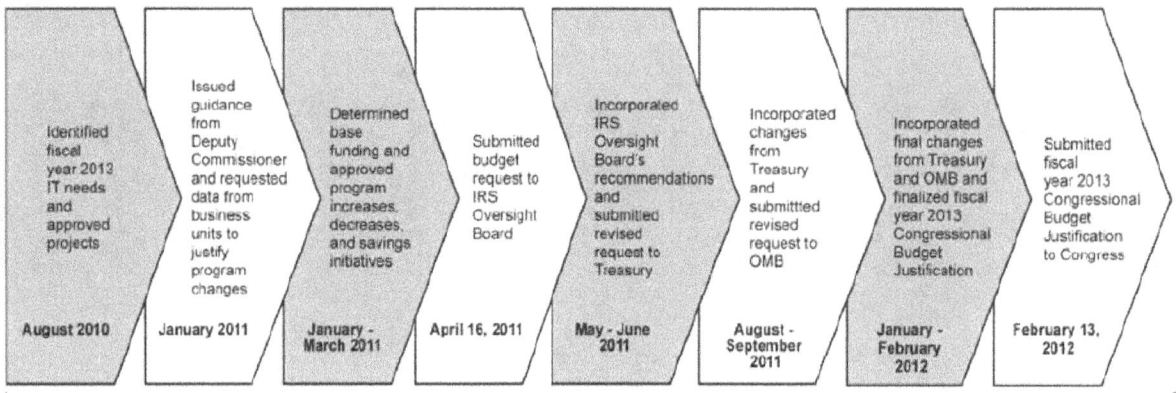

Changes, reductions, or additions are made at every stage of the budget process.

Source: GAO analysis of IRS data.

Page 8

Background

IRS Funding for PPACA

* Congress passed PPACA[1] in March 2010 to reform the private insurance market and expand health coverage to the uninsured. IRS is responsible for implementing new provisions including new taxes, tax credits, and information reporting requirements.

* Subsequently, Congress established the Health Insurance Reform Implementation Fund (HIRIF)[2] within the Department of Health and Human Services (HHS) for federal administrative expenses in carrying out PPACA.

* Congress appropriated $1 billion to the HIRIF. IRS was one of the agencies eligible to use this appropriation to fund PPACA implementation.

    * HHS provided $188.9 million/609 FTEs to IRS from HIRIF in fiscal year 2010 ($20.7 million/33 FTEs) and fiscal year 2011 ($168.2 million/576 FTEs).

[1] Pub. L. No. 111-148, 124 Stat. 119 (Mar. 23, 2010).
[2] Health Care and Education Reconciliation Act of 2010, Pub. L. No. 111-152, 124 Stat. 1029 (Mar. 30, 2010).

Page 9

Fiscal Year 2012 Funding Reductions

Fiscal Year 2012 Enacted IRS Appropriations Reduced by $305 Million (2.5 Percent) from Fiscal Year 2011

• Most fiscal year 2012 reductions (in terms of dollars) were in the Enforcement and Operations Support appropriations.
• IRS requested $473.4 million (1,269 FTEs) for PPACA in fiscal year 2012, but it was not funded. Subsequently, IRS received $135.4 million from HIRIF through March 31, 2012. Officials anticipate requesting an additional $196.8 million, totaling $332.2 million (803 FTEs) from HIRIF for fiscal year 2012.

Table 1: Funding Reductions in IRS's Appropriations between Fiscal Year 2011 and Fiscal Year 2012 (dollars in millions)

	Fiscal year 2011 enacted	Fiscal year 2012 enacted	Dollar change (percent change) fiscal year 2011 to fiscal year 2012
Enforcement	$5,493	$5,299	-$194 (-3.5%)
Operations support	4,057	3,947	-109 (-2.7)
Taxpayer services	2,293	2,240	-54 (-2.3)
BSM	263	330	67 (25.4)
Health Insurance Tax Credit Administration (HITCA)	15	0a	-15 (-100.0)
Total appropriated resources	$12,122	$11,817	-$305 (-2.5%)

Source: Fiscal year 2013 Congressional Budget Justification for IRS.
Note: Numbers may not add due to rounding.
a In fiscal year 2012, administrative resources for HITCA were moved to the Taxpayer Services appropriation under the Consolidated Appropriations Act, 2012 (Pub. L. No. 112-74).

Page 10

Fiscal Year 2012 Funding Reductions

IRS Decreased FTEs and Other Costs, but Did Not Fully Implement GAO's Recommendation to Systematically Re-Examine Base Operations

- To manage the reductions to its appropriations, IRS:
  - Decreased FTEs by at least 3.4 percent[1] from fiscal year 2011 through use of attrition, a hiring freeze, and targeted buyouts of more than 900 staff.
    - After receiving HIRIF funding for staffing (227 FTEs), the net decrease in FTEs was 3.1 percent.
  - Reduced other costs through cuts to travel, training, consulting services, IT investments, and increased use of telework and video conferencing.

- IRS officials said they examined base operations at a high level, but did not provide us documentation of their analysis. IRS's officials also said that spending reductions were focused on minimizing the impact on services to taxpayers and operations.
  - We previously recommended IRS expand efforts to systematically identify savings and efficiencies as part of its budget development process.[2]
  - IRS may be missing opportunities to realize savings and efficiencies by not fully reviewing base operations.

[1]Reduction in FTEs calculated from fiscal year 2011 actual and fiscal year 2012 enacted FTE levels.
[2]GAO, IRS Budget 2012: Extending Systematic Reviews of Spending Could Identify More Savings Over Time, GAO-11-547 (Washington, D.C.: Apr. 11, 2011).

Page 11

Fiscal Year 2012 Funding Reductions

Selected Measures Show Declines in Performance or Planned Targets for Some Taxpayer Service and Enforcement Activities Since Fiscal Year 2007

Table 2: Selected Taxpayer Service and Enforcement Measures for Fiscal Year 2007 through Fiscal Year 2013

Performance measure (in percent)	Fiscal year 2007 (actual)	Fiscal year 2008 (actual)	Fiscal year 2009 (actual)	Fiscal year 2010 (actual)	Fiscal year 2011 (actual)	Fiscal year 2012 (planned target)	Fiscal year 2013 (planned target)
Assistor calls –							
Level of service[a]	82.1	52.8	70.0	74.0	70.1	61.0	63.0
Tax law accuracy[b]	91.2	91.2	92.9	92.7	93.4	92.7	92.7
Account accuracy[b]	93.4	93.7	94.9	95.7	96.0	95.0	95.0
Examination coverage—individual[c]	1.0	1.0	1.0	1.1	1.1	1.0	1.0
Examination coverage—business[c] (assets > $10 million)	6.8	6.1	5.6	5.7	6.2	5.6	5.4
Collection coverage[d]	54.0	55.2	54.2	50.1	50.0	47.8	46.8

Source: Fiscal Year 2013 Congressional Budget Justification for IRS.

[a] The number of toll-free callers that speak to live IRS assistors divided by the total number of attempted calls.

[b] Accuracy measures show how often customers receives the correct answer/solution to their inquiry from a live IRS assistor.

[c] Examination coverage is the number of tax returns examined and closed during the current fiscal year divided by the number of returns for the preceding year.

[d] Collection coverage measures the volume of collection work completed compared to the volume of collection work available.

Page 12

Fiscal Year 2012 Funding Reductions

IRS's Telephone Level of Service in Fiscal Year 2012 Has Decreased

- As of mid-April 2012, the telephone level of service[1] was 68.3 percent, down 6.3 percentage points compared to the same period last year.
  - At the enacted funding level, the planned target for fiscal year 2012 is 61 percent, down from its target of 82 percent for fiscal year 2008.

- Hours assistors are available to answer calls decreased 20 percent from fiscal year 2011, from 15 hours to 12 hours per day. Average wait times to talk with an assistor during the same period increased from 9.9 minutes to 15.8 minutes.

- Abandoned, busy, and disconnected calls are up more than 26 percent during the same period in 2011 and are up almost 67 percent from the same period in 2008.

[1]Level of service is the number of toll-free callers that speak to live IRS assistors divided by the total number of attempted calls.

Page 13

Fiscal Year 2012 Funding Reductions

New Tax Laws Increase IRS's Responsibilities

- Several new laws could substantially increase IRS's workload beginning in 2012; for example:

  - In fiscal year 2011, IRS received 1.8 billion information returns.[1] Three new laws require (1) brokers to report the adjusted cost basis for certain securities and identify whether a gain or loss is short or long-term,[2] (2) merchants to report the gross amount of income from payment card or third-party payment network transactions,[3] and (3) foreign banks to provide information on taxpayer accounts via the Foreign Account Tax Compliance Act (FATCA).[4] IRS's fiscal year 2012 and fiscal year 2013 information return projections increase to 2.5 billion and 2.6 billion, respectively.

  - In addition to processing increased information reports, IRS will also have other responsibilities related to FATCA, such as identifying filers not complying with FATCA requirements and imposing tax penalties when necessary.

  - For PPACA, IRS has several new responsibilities, such as administering new fees on drug manufacturers and health insurers, processing newly required reports, and reviewing the community benefit activities of tax-exempt hospitals, which they need to prepare for and implement over the next several years.

[1]Information returns are tax documents third parties are required to file to RS that report certain transactions, such as interest earned from a bank account.
[2]Energy Improvement and Extension Act of 2008, Pub. L. No. 110-343, div. B, § 403, 122 Stat. 3765, 3854-3860 (Oct. 3, 2008).

[3]Housing Assistance Tax Act of 2008, Pub. L. No. 110-289, div. C, § 3091, 122 Stat. 2654, 2908-2911 (July 30, 2008).
[4]Hiring Incentives to Restore Employment Act, Pub. L. No. 111-147, title V, 124 Stat. 71, 97-117 (Mar. 18, 2010).

Page 14

Fiscal Year 2012 Funding Reductions

Opportunities Exist to Increase Efficiencies and More Strategically Manage Operations

- In recent reports, we highlighted opportunities for IRS to modify its current operations to improve taxpayer services and enforcement programs, which could aid IRS by providing savings over time. For example:
  - providing more automated services (GAO-12-176);
  - conducting more pre-refund compliance checks through broadening use of Math Error Authority (GAO-10-349, GAO-10-225);
  - using data from new information returns effectively (GAO-11-557);
  - leveraging paid tax preparers (GAO-12-652T, GAO-11-336); and
  - increasing availability of electronic data (GAO-12-33).

- These reports provide recommendations to increase efficiencies and manage operations more strategically. However, some may require upfront investments before the efficiencies can be fully realized.

Page 15

Fiscal Year 2013 Budget Data and Trends

Summary of Key Budget and FTE Data

- The fiscal year 2013 budget request proposes:
  - a $944.5 million (8.0 percent) increase over fiscal year 2012, with the Enforcement and Operations Support appropriations accounting for the largest increase.
    - The fiscal year 2013 request is an increase of 5.3 percent over fiscal year 2011.
    - Of the $944.5 million, $360.5 million is for PPACA-related implementation, to be funded from IRS's appropriations. IRS officials expect the HIRIF funds will not available for use in fiscal year 2013.
  - a Taxpayer Service appropriation at about the same level as last year.
    - IRS expects to gain savings and efficiencies from more electronically filed returns and other program reductions.
  - a net increase of about 4,500 (5.0 percent) FTEs over fiscal year 2012.
    - The largest requested increase for FTEs is for Enforcement.
    - Of the 4,500 FTEs, 859 are for PPACA, including 803 FTEs which IRS officials told us were on-board and funded by HIRIF in fiscal year 2012.

Page 16

Fiscal Year 2013 Budget Data and Trends

Dollars by Appropriation Account, Fiscal Year 2008 through Fiscal Year 2013

Table 3: Fiscal Year 2008 through Fiscal Year 2012 Enacted and Fiscal Year 2013 Budget Request for IRS by Appropriation Account (dollars in millions)

Appropriation Account	Fiscal year 2008 enacted	Fiscal year 2009 enacted	Fiscal year 2010 enacted	Fiscal year 2011 enacted	Fiscal year 2012 enacted	Fiscal year 2013 requested	Dollar change fiscal year 2012 enacted compared to fiscal year 2013 requested	Percent change fiscal year 2012 enacted compared to fiscal year 2013 requested
Enforcement	$4,780	$5,117	$5,504	$5,493	$5,299	$5,702	$403	7.59
Operations support	3,841	3,867	4,084	4,057	3,947	4,476	529	13.40
Taxpayer services	2,191	2,293	2,279	2,293	2,240	2,253	13	0.60
BSM	267	230	264	263	330	330	0	0.00
HITCA	15	15	16	15	-- a	-- a	-- a	-- a
Subtotal	11,095	11,523	12,146	12,122	11,817	12,761	945	7.99
Other resources, such as user fees[b]	566	390	539	655	559	592	34	6.04
Total funding available for obligation[c]	$11,661	$11,913	$12,686	$12,777	$12,375	$13,354	$979	7.91

Source: Fiscal Year 2010 through Fiscal Year 2013 Congressional Budget Justifications for RS.

Notes: Dollars are nominal and not adjusted for inflation, and numbers may not add due to rounding.

[a]In fiscal year 2012, administrative resources for HITCA were moved to the Taxpayer Services appropriation under the Consolidated Appropriations Act, 2012 (Pub. L. No. 112-74).

[b]Other resources available for obligation are estimated by IRS and not subject to the annual appropriations process.

[c] RS received an additional $20.7 million in fiscal year 2010 and $168.2 million in fiscal year 2011 from HHS's H RIF fund to implement PPACA. In fiscal year 2012, RS plans to request $332.2 million from HHS and had received $135.4 million through March 31, 2012. RS officials do not anticipate requesting HHS funds in fiscal year 2013, and have requested $360.5 million through RS's appropriation for fiscal year 2013.

Page 17

Fiscal Year 2013 Budget Data and Trends
Staffing by Appropriation Account, Fiscal Year 2008 through Fiscal Year 2013

Table 4: Fiscal Year 2008 through Fiscal Year 2011 Actual, Fiscal Year 2012 Enacted, and Fiscal Year 2013 Requested FTEs by Appropriation Account

Appropriation account	Fiscal year 2008 actual	Fiscal year 2009 actual	Fiscal year 2010 actual	Fiscal year 2011 actual[a]	Fiscal year 2012 enacted	Fiscal year 2013 requested	FTE change fiscal year 2012 enacted compared to fiscal year 2013 requested	Percent change fiscal year 2012 enacted compared to fiscal year 2013 requested
Enforcement	46,431	47,361	50,400	49,920	47,586	51,583	3,997	8.40
Operations support	12,079	12,101	12,262	12,103	11,985	12,609	624	5.21
Taxpayer services	31,487	32,422	31,607	31,574	30,535	30,570	35	0.11
BSM	347	322	337	309	605	495	-110	-18.18
HITCA[b]	10	10	12	0	0	0	0	0
Subtotal	90,354	92,216	94,618	93,906	90,711	95,257	4,546	5.01
Other resources, such as user fees[c]	1,331	1,153	752	1,003	939	939	0	0
Total FTEs[d]	91,685	93,369	95,370	94,909	91,650	96,196	4,546	4.96

Source: Fiscal Year 2008 through Fiscal Year 2013 Congressional Budget Justifications for RS.

[a] RS reported both enacted and actual FTEs for fiscal year 2011 in the fiscal year 2013 Congressional Budget Justification. For purposes of this table, we reported actual amounts.
[b] The administrative resources for HITCA were moved to the Taxpayer Services appropriation under the Consolidated Appropriations Act, 2012 (Pub. L. No. 112-74).
[c] Other resources available for obligation are estimated by RS and not subject to the annual appropriations process.
[d] RS realized an additional 33 FTEs in fiscal year 2010, 576 FTEs in fiscal year 2011, and is projecting 227 more FTEs for fiscal year 2012, for a cumulative total of 803 FTEs to be funded from HIR F, according to RS officials. The budget for fiscal year 2013 requested an additional 56 FTEs to make the cumulative total 859 FTEs. For fiscal year 2013, the budget proposes to fund the entire 859 FTEs from RS's appropriation, and not H RIF.

Page 18

Fiscal Year 2013 Budget Data and Trends

Of the $945 Million Requested Increase, the Administration Proposed a Program Integrity Cap Adjustment for Increases in IRS Enforcement and Compliance Funding

- Congress passes program integrity cap adjustments to allow additional funding above discretionary spending limits for certain activities that are expected to generate benefits that exceed cost.

- The Administration requested a cap adjustment of $691 million for IRS in fiscal year 2013.

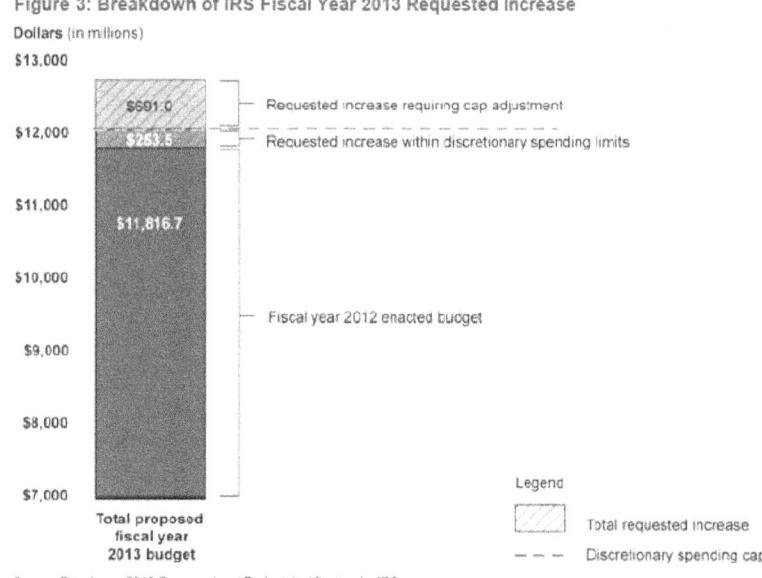

Figure 3: Breakdown of IRS Fiscal Year 2013 Requested Increase

Dollars (in millions)

- $691.0 — Requested increase requiring cap adjustment
- $253.5 — Requested increase within discretionary spending limits
- $11,816.7 — Fiscal year 2012 enacted budget

Total proposed fiscal year 2013 budget

Legend

▨ Total requested increase

– – – Discretionary spending cap

Source: Fiscal year 2013 Congressional Budget Justification for IRS.

Page 19

Fiscal Year 2013 Budget Data and Trends
Breakout of $945 Million Requested Increase

Table 5: Funding Requested for New Initiatives and Changes Due to Inflation, Pay Raises, and Savings and Efficiencies (dollars in millions)

Description of new initiatives		Fiscal year 2013 funding requested	Subtotal	Total
Total changes				$1,015.3
New initiatives			906.9	
Enforcement initiatives	Restore audit and collection coverage to address individual tax compliance issues (Projected ROI: 6.8 to 1. IRS's ROI estimate is based on direct revenues collected and does not include revenue that may result from an increase in voluntary compliance.)	200 5		
	Implement tax law changes for Information Reporting and Document Matching (RDM) and PPACA programs (Projected ROI: 3.5 to 1).	128 9		
	Promote offshore compliance (Projected ROI: 6.4 to 1).	110.7		
	Implement revenue protection strategy (Projected ROI: 1.9 to 1).	88 9		
	Other (improve international compliance, build out return preparer program, address appeals workload, leverage digital evidence, and implement uncertain tax position reporting requirements) (Unable to provide ROI because not all initiatives are revenue generating.)	102 9		
Infrastructure initiatives	To implement PPACA-related IT and operational infrastructure to allow IRS to validate household income and determine the amount of advance payments of the tax credit.	275.1		
Inflation adjustment and pay raises	Inflation adjustments for non-labor expenses such as rent, postage, and health benefits, in order to maintain current levels and a proposed pay raise of 0.5 percent.		108.4	
Savings and efficiencies	Savings resulting from targeted program reductions ($59.7 million, e.g., using more online tools and IT contractual services), increased use of electronic filing of returns ($8.6 million), and reduced travel ($2.6 million).			-70.9
Appropriation increase				$944.5

Source: Fiscal Year 2013 Congressional Budget Justification for RS.
Note: Numbers may not add due to rounding.

Page 20

New Initiatives and ROI

7 of the 12 Proposed New Enforcement Initiatives ($603.1 Million) Supported with ROIs[1]

Figure 4: Implement Tax Legislative Changes

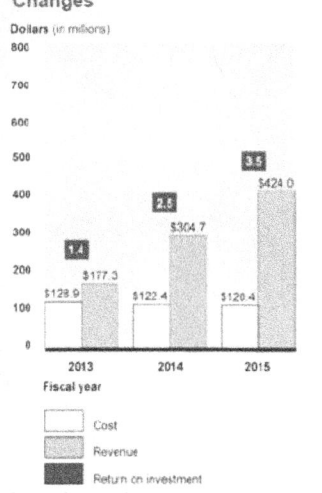

Figure 5: Restore Audit Coverage to Address Individual Tax Compliance

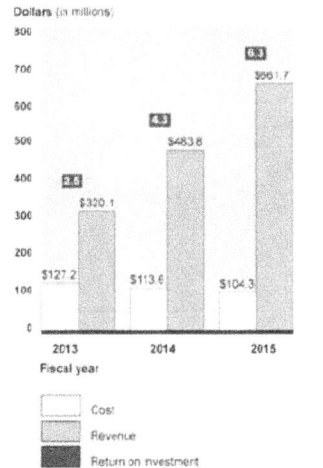

Figure 6: Promote Offshore Compliance

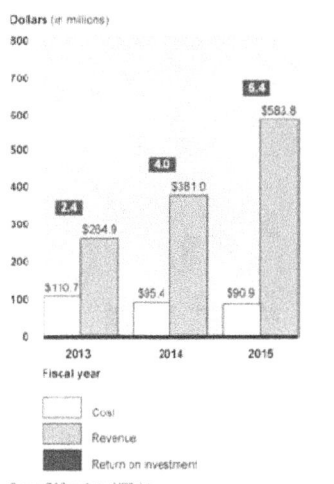

Implement RDM (2015 ROI: 7.5 to 1) and PPACA (2015 ROI: 1.8 to 1). Related GAO work: GAO-12-59, GAO-11-719, GAO-11-557.

Increases for audit and individual compliance programs, such as correspondence exams of refundable credits, the global high wealth strategy, two-dimensional barcoding, and document imaging. Related GAO work: GAO-12-33.

Address FATCA requirements, strengthen offshore enforcement, and develop related IT. Related GAO work: GAO-11-730, GAO-11-493, GAO-11-272, GAO-09-478T, GAO-08-99, GAO-08-778.

[1]IRS's ROI calculations have limitations that reflect the challenges of estimating ROIs. For example, they do not include benefits of improved voluntary compliance. In addition, the "investment" or costs should ideally recognize not just IRS costs, but any costs borne by others. IRS's ROI estimates provide useful information but, given the limits of current data, are not complete estimates of benefits and costs.

Page 21

New Initiatives and ROI

7 of the 12 Proposed New Enforcement Initiatives ($603.1 Million) Supported with ROIs[1] (continued)

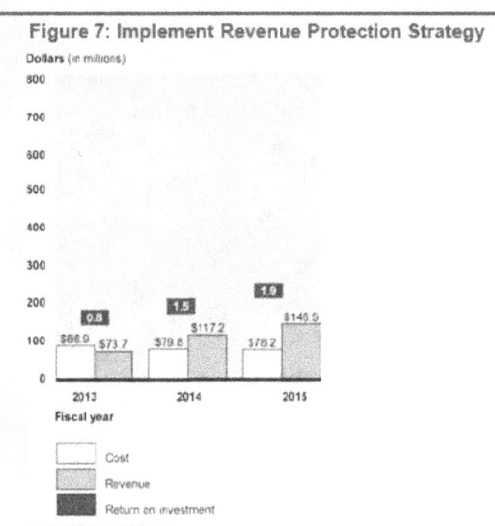

Figure 7: Implement Revenue Protection Strategy

Prevent erroneous refunds through four programs (return review, management taxpayer assurance, identity theft, and prisoner tax compliance) Related GAO work: GAO-11-721T, GAO-11-691T, GAO-11-674T, GAO-09-882, GAO-02-363.

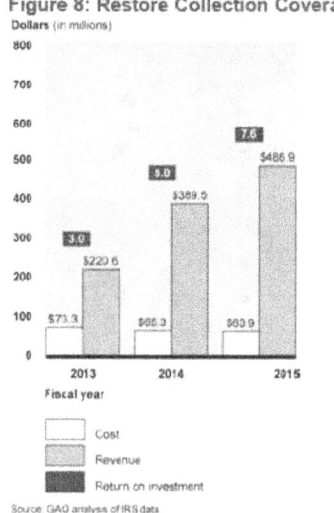

Figure 8: Restore Collection Coverage

Increases for collection coverage such as staffing for Automated Collection Systems, Offers in Compromise, and Accounts Management programs. Related GAO work: GAO-06-525.

[1]IRS's ROI calculations have limitations that reflect the challenges of estimating ROIs. For example, they do not include benefits of improved voluntary compliance. In addition, the "investment" or costs should ideally recognize not just IRS costs, but any costs borne by others. IRS's ROI estimates provide useful information but, given the limits of current data, are not complete estimates of benefits and costs.

Page 22

New Initiatives and ROI

7 of the 12 Proposed New Enforcement Initiatives ($603.1 Million) Supported with ROIs[1] (continued)

Figure 9: Improve International Compliance

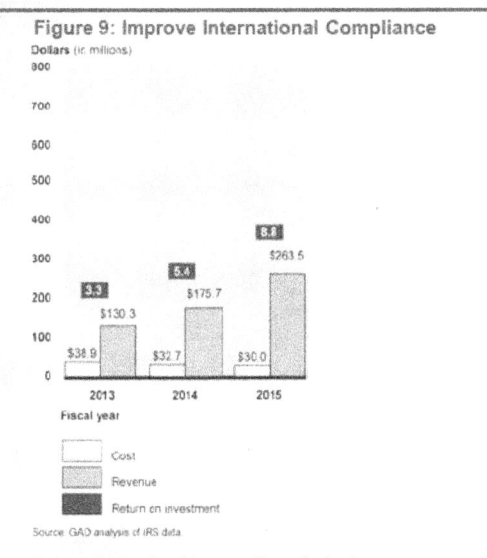

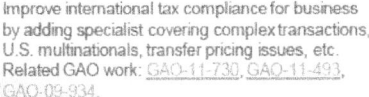

Source: GAO analysis of IRS data

Improve international tax compliance for business by adding specialist covering complex transactions, U.S. multinationals, transfer pricing issues, etc. Related GAO work: GAO-11-730, GAO-11-493, GAO-09-934.

Figure 10: Build Out Tax Return Preparer Program

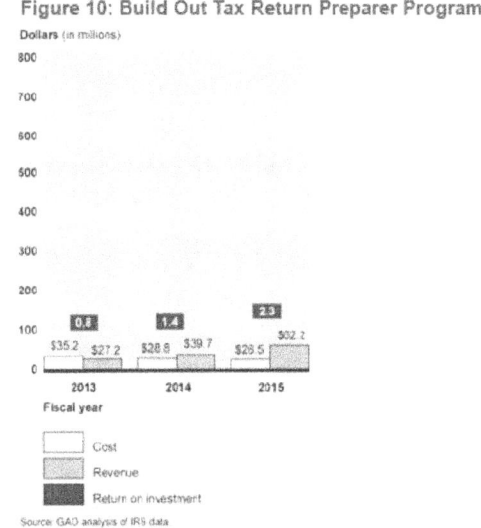

Source: GAO analysis of IRS data

Enforce compliance, pursue fraud, educate preparers and enforce ethical standards. Related GAO work: GAO-11-868T, GAO-11-336, GAO-06-563T, GAO-03-610T, Podcast, "Regulation of Tax Preparation and Filing."

[1]IRS's ROI calculations have limitations that reflect the challenges of estimating ROIs. For example, they do not include benefits of improved voluntary compliance. In addition, the "investment" or costs should ideally recognize not just IRS costs, but any costs borne by others. IRS's ROI estimates provide useful information but, given the limits of current data, are not complete estimates of benefits and costs.

Page 23

New Initiatives and ROI

Some New Initiatives Were Not Supported by Economic Analysis

• We examined 2 of the 5 new initiatives without ROIs, the ones pertaining to the PPACA mandate, which totaled $275.1 million.

    •IRS did not estimate ROIs for these 5 new initiatives because they do not generate enforcement revenue. However, IRS did not justify them with any other similar economic analyses, such as a cost-effectiveness analysis, which compares costs of alternative means of achieving the same benefit.

Table 6: Purpose and Related GAO Work, Estimated Cost, and Basis for New Initiatives without ROI (in millions)

Initiative	Purpose (related GAO work)	Estimated fiscal year 2013 cost (FTE)	Basis of initiative
Implement IT and operational infrastructure to deliver PPACA	Develop new and modify/enhance of new and existing IT systems to administer the PPACA. (GAO-11-719)	$266.9 (537)	Mandated
Address appeals workload	Add 92 settlement officers and 40 appeals officers to handle rising appeals workload.	20 3 (132)	IRS-initiated
Implement IT changes needed for individual coverage for PPACA	For contractor to develop IT, infrastructure, and systems to implement individual responsibility health coverage requirement of PPACA. (GAO-11-719)	8 2 (0)	Mandated
Leverage digital evidence for Criminal Investigation (CI)	Implement "virtual digital evidence processing environment" that will allow CI to expedite and improve analysis of electronic data and avoid travel costs.	4 5 (8)	IRS-initiated
Implement uncertain tax position reporting requirements	Increase IRS capacity to provide guidance and certainty on areas of legal uncertainty for large business taxpayers, e.g., advanced pricing agreements and private letter rulings.	4.0 (20)	IRS-initiated
Total		$303.9 (697)	

Source: GAO analysis of IRS's Fiscal Year 2013 Congressional Budget Justification for RS.

Page 24

New Initiatives and ROI

Alternatives to Implement PPACA Initiatives Considered, but Not Potential Costs

- At the time the PPACA mandate was imposed, IRS considered alternative approaches for implementing it, but did not consider the costs of the alternatives. The analyses did consider other factors, such as risk to the agency and time. We have previously reported on the need for IRS to conduct economic analyses.[1]

- Sound cost-effectiveness analyses demonstrate that different approaches were evaluated, according to OMB *Circular A-94*. They also provide assurance that the alternatives chosen were the most cost effective and, if not, why. A cost-effectiveness analysis is itself an investment, so the level of detail should be commensurate with the magnitude of the initiative.

- Officials said they did not determine the costs of all PPACA alternatives. They said they normally develop cost estimates only for the alternative they plan to implement.

- When comparisons of alternatives do not consider costs, budget decision makers cannot be assured that alternatives were fully evaluated and the best alternative, based on factors including cost, was selected.

[1]GAO, *Tax Debt Collection: IRS Could Improve Future Studies by Establishing Appropriate Guidance*, GAO-10-963 (Washington, D.C.: Sept. 24, 2010).

Page 25

PPACA Cost Estimate

PPACA Cost Estimate Partially Met Best Practices for Reliability, but Has Not Been Updated Since 2010

- IRS developed a cost estimate for PPACA in October 2010. However, it did not fully meet best practices for a reliable cost estimate, including containing timely updates to ensure accuracy. We alerted IRS to this issue in June 2011. Since then, IRS has not updated its cost estimate (see appendix III for a full description of our assessment of IRS's PPACA cost estimate).

- Cost estimates establish and defend budgets. They are integral to determining and communicating a realistic view of likely cost and schedule outcomes that can be used to plan the work necessary to develop, produce, install, and support a program. Best practices for a reliable cost estimate are outlined in our *Cost Guide*.[1] In particular, we note the importance of updated and timely cost estimates that are available to decision makers as early as possible.

[1]GAO-09-3SP

Page 26

PPACA Cost Estimate

PPACA Cost Estimate Partially Met Best Practices for Reliability, but Has Not Been Updated Since 2010 (continued)

- IRS officials told us cost estimates are updated after projects reach particular milestones. The last milestone for PPACA was reached in January 2012. IRS awarded a contract to update the PPACA cost estimate on April 26, 2012. The contract specifies that the updated cost estimate should follow GAO best practices for a comprehensive, well documented, accurate, and credible cost estimate. IRS officials expect that the updated cost estimate will be completed by August or September 2012.

- Until the update is completed, budget decision makers may not have sufficient information to consider trade-offs for fiscal year 2013 budget deliberations. For example, they will not know the fraction of the multi-year PPACA effort being funded in fiscal year 2013 and therefore will not know the costs that remain to be funded in future years.

Page 27

Budgeting for New Staff

Budgeting Practices Could Result in Funding Being Used for Other Purposes

- IRS budgets for staff for new initiatives assuming an October 1 start date, but in recent years, it hired most new staff late in the fiscal year. During fiscal year 2009 and fiscal year 2010, the last years IRS received new initiative funding, most new staff started in the 3rd or 4th quarter, as shown in figure 11.

- While partly due to the timing of enacted budgets, IRS's hiring pattern is also due to practical limitations in hiring and training large numbers of staff. For example, IRS significantly planned and prepared for a large hiring wave in fiscal year 2009, when it brought on about 1,500 new employees in three waves over a 9 month period.[1]

- With congressional approval, IRS can use funding budgeted for new staff for other purposes within limits.[2]

- Based on recent hiring trends for new initiatives, we estimate about $300 million of planned funding for FTEs in fiscal year 2013 could be used for other purposes, subject to congressional approval, and are not described or substantiated in the budget.

Figure 11: Actual Hiring for New Permanent Staff for New Initiatives by Quarter, Fiscal Year 2009 through Fiscal Year 2010

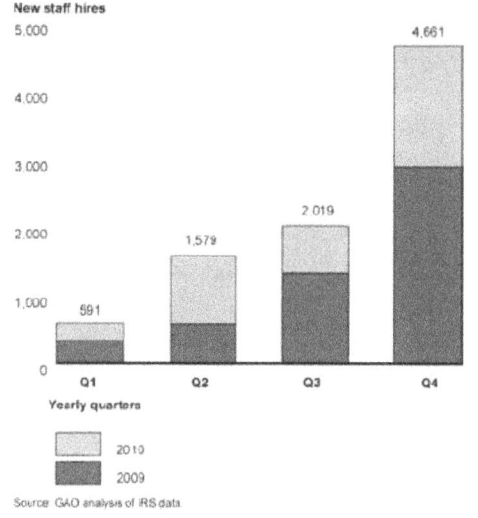

[1]Treasury Inspector General for Tax Administration, *Challenges Remain to Balance Revenue Officer Staffing With Attrition and Workload Demands*, TIGTA 2011-30-039 (Washington, D.C.: May 6, 2011).

[2] RS can transfer funds between appropriations, but those transfers cannot exceed 5 percent of any appropriation or 3 percent of the Enforcement appropriation.

Page 28

Budgeting for New Staff

Budgeting Practices Could Result in Funding Being Used for Other Purposes (continued)

- We have previously reported that budgets should be transparent, meaning that are made clear, salient, and understandable to decision makers and the public.[1] Budget transparency is critical for effective congressional oversight and decision making. OMB *Circular A-11* suggests agencies consider delays in recruiting and hiring and actual compensable number of hours worked when budgeting for staff.

- According to IRS and OMB officials, there is an agreement between the two agencies dating from the 1990s that permits IRS to budget for new staff assuming full year costs. According to officials, this practice helps IRS ensure it has full funding available for the newly hired staff in the second year without the need to justify a budget increase and manage uncertainties due to delays in funding.
  - Neither IRS nor OMB officials were able to provide us with written documentation of the agreement. OMB officials said that they commonly make informal, oral agreements with agencies as part of the budget process and that *Circular A-11* allows for some flexibility.

- Providing substantiation that fully identified planned uses for funding that result from hiring later in the year could increase transparency and aid Congress in making difficult resource decisions.

[1]GAO, *Internal Revenue Service: Assessment of Budget Justification for Fiscal Year 2011 Identified Opportunities to Enhance Transparency,* GAO-10-687R (Washington, D.C.: May 26, 2010), and GAO, *Budget Issues: Budgeting for Federal Insurance Programs,* GAO/T-AIMD-98-147 (Washington, D.C.: April 23, 1998).

Page 29

IT Investments

IT Is About 20 Percent of IRS's Fiscal Year 2013 Budget Request

- IRS requested about $2.5 billion for IT for fiscal year 2013—$330 million for BSM and $2.14 billion for other investments.

    - Of the $2.5 billion requested,
        - $1.6 billion is planned to fund 18 major investments[1] and
        - $900 million is planned to fund 125 non-major investments.

- For fiscal year 2012, IRS has 20 major IT investments[2] for which cost and schedule information and Treasury CIO ratings are reported to OMB on a monthly basis (see appendix IV for a description of the major investments). The CIO's evaluation is based on a number of factors to forecast the future success of the investment.

[1]According to RS, major investments are defined by Treasury as those that cost $10 million in either current year or budget year, or $50 million over the 5 year period extending from the prior year through budget year +2.

[2] RS eliminated two major investments in the fiscal year 2013 budget request.

Page 30

IT Investments

IRS's Major Investments and Estimated IT Costs

Table 7: IRS's 20 Major Investments and Estimated IT Costs for Fiscal Year 2011 through Fiscal Year 2016 (in millions)

Investment name	Total estimated development costs	Total estimated operations and maintenance costs	Total estimated government FTE costs	Total estimated costs
Account Management Services (AMS)	$0 0	$43.0	$60.2	$103.2
Affordable Care Act (ACA) Administration[a]	303 5	0.0	0.0	303 5[b]
Current Customer Account Data Engine (CADE)[c]	557 5	116.0	22.8	696.3
CADE 2	852.7	0.2	295.0	1,148.0
Electronic Fraud Detection System (EFDS)	0 0	59.6	18.1	77.7
e-Services (e-SVS)	28.7	34.3	19.5	82.5
Foreign Account Tax Compliance Act (FATCA)	23 9	8.5	9.9	42.3
Implement Return Review Program (RRP) (Replaces EFDS)	72 2	8.4	6.8	87.3
Individual Master File (MF)	0 0	22.3	49.1	71.4
Information Reporting and Document Matching (RDM)	54 8	6.6	49.4	110.8
Integrated Customer Communication Environment (ICCE)	16 2	29.8	43.3	89.3
Integrated Data Retrieval System (IDRS)	0 0	23.0	266.9	290.0
Integrated Financial System/CORE Financial System (FS)	13 2	73.1	8.5	94.9
Integrated Submission and Remittance Processing System (ISRP)	1 3	65.2	13.8	80.3
IRS End User Systems and Services (EUSS)	0 0	585.1	892.1	1,477.3
IRS Main Frames and Servers Services and Support (MSSS)	0 0	4,033.7	0.0	4,033.7
IRS Telecommunications Systems and Support (TSS)	0 0	1,432.9	322.3	1,755.1
IRS.GOV - Portal Environment[d]	320 0	244.0	564.0	1,128.0
Modernized e-File (MeF)	184 8	54.4	52.9	292.1
Service Center Recognition/Image Processing System (SCRIPS)	1 0	56.0	11.3	68.3
Total	$2,429.9	$6,896.3	$2,705.9	$12,032.0

Source: GAO analysis of IRS's Exhibit 300A data.

Note: Numbers may not add due to rounding.

[a]IRS is implementing PPACA requirements under the investment name of ACA, and funding through the end of fiscal year 2012 is from HIRIF.

[b]This amount only represents IT estimates for fiscal year 2013 because we did not receive actual fiscal year 2011 costs from IRS in time to include them. We also did not receive IT estimates for fiscal year 2012, fiscal year 2014, fiscal year 2015, and fiscal year 2016 from IRS in time to include them.

[c]According to IRS, the Current CADE Investment ended on December 31, 2011. The costs represent life-cycle costs consistent with how costs are reported to OMB for this investment.

[d]The costs represent life-cycle costs consistent with how costs are reported to OMB for this investment.

Page 31

IT Investments

Performance of IRS's Major IT Investments

- According to IRS, most major IT investments were generally within cost and schedule estimates between October 2011 and March 2012[1] and Treasury CIO ratings showed that most major IT investments were moderately low risk in recent months. However, we could not determine whether these investments delivered planned functionality.
- IRS reported that, between October 2011 and March 2012,
  - 14 of the 20 major IT investments were within 10 percent of cost and schedule estimates.
  - the remaining 6 investments reported significant variances from cost or schedule estimates.[2] Significant variances are typically analyzed to determine root causes, as they may indicate problems needing corrective actions (see appendix V).
    - Over cost estimate: Current CADE and MeF
    - Over schedule estimate: ISRP and MSSS
    - Under cost estimate: ACA[3] and ICCE

[1]Based on changes to OMB budget guidance, IRS adopted a new methodology for reporting on cost and schedule performance for its major IT investments, starting October 2011. Given these changes, we are reporting from October 2011 to March 2012.

[2]A significant variance from cost and/or schedule is defined as anything below or exceeds 10 percent.
[3]IRS is implementing PPACA requirements under the investment name of ACA.

Page 32

IT Investments

CIO Rated 17 Investments at Moderately Low or Low Risk in Recent Months

• The CIO rating shows how the Treasury CIO viewed the performance of each investment during a rating period.

• This rating is based on risk management, requirements management, contract or oversight, historical performance, human capital, or any other factors that the CIO deems important to forecasting the future success of the investment.

Table 8: CIO Rated Major IT Investments

Investment Name	Mar-11	Apr-11	May-11	Jun-11	Jul-11	Aug-11[b]	Sep-11[b]	Oct-11	Nov-11	Dec-11	Jan-12	Feb-12	Mar-12
Account Management Services (AMS)	4	4	N/A	4	3	N/A	N/A	4	4	4	4	4	4
Affordable Care Act Administration (ACA)[a]								N/A	N/A	N/A	N/A	N/A	4[c]
Current Customer Account Data Engine (CADE)	4	4	4	4	3	N/A	N/A	5	5	5	5	5	5
CADE 2	4	4	4	4	4	N/A	N/A	4	4	4	4	4	4
Electronic Fraud Detection System (EFDS)	4	4	4	5	5	N/A	N/A	4	4	4	4	4	4
e-Services (e-SVS)	4	4	5	5	5	N/A	N/A	4	4	4	4	4	4
Foreign Account Tax Compliance Act (FATCA)[a]								N/A	N/A	N/A	N/A	4	4
Implement RRP (Replaces EFDS)	3	3	3	3	4	N/A	N/A	4	3	3	3	3	3
Individual Master File (IMF)	4	4	4	4	4	N/A	N/A	4	4	4	4	4	4
Information Reporting and Document Matching (IRDM)	2	2	2	2	2	N/A	N/A	4	4	4	4	4	4
Integrated Customer Communication Environment (ICCE)	4	4	4	4	4	N/A	N/A	4	4	4	4	4	4
Integrated Data Retrieval System (IDRS)	5	5	5	5	5	N/A	N/A	5	5	5	5	5	5
Integrated Financial System/CORE Financial System (IFS)	3	3	5	5	5	N/A	N/A	4	4	4	4	4	4
Integrated Submission and Remittance Processing System (ISRP)	5	5	5	5	5	N/A	N/A	5	5	5	5	5	5
IRS End User Systems and Services (EUSS)[a]								4	4	4	4	4	4
IRS Main Frames and Servers Services and Support (MSSS)[a]								4	4	5	3	3	3
IRS Telecommunications Systems and Support (TSS)[a]								4	4	4	4	4	4
IRS GOV Portal Environment	3	3	3	3	3	N/A	N/A	4	4	4	4	4	4
Modernized e-File (MeF)	4	4	3	3	5	N/A	N/A	4	4	4	4	4	4
Service Center Recognition/Image Processing System (SCRIPS)	4	4	4	4	4	N/A	N/A	5	5	5	5	5	5

2: Moderately High Risk   3: Medium Risk   4: Moderately Low Risk   5: Low Risk

Source: GAO analysis of IRS's data and OMB's Dashboard.

[a] These investments were not reported on the IT dashboard until it was designated a major IT investment in October 2011.
[b] According to IRS, CIO ratings for August and September 2011 were not available because of the transition period to newer cost and schedule calculations.
[c] Because HHS has overall responsibility for ACA, IRS does not provide separate reports to OMB on this investment. We did not obtain the CIO rating information prior to March 2012 from HHS in time for this review.

Page 33

IT Investments

IRS Does Not Have a Quantitative Measure of Scope

- While IRS reports on the cost and schedule of its major investments and provides CIO ratings for them, the agency does not have a quantitative measure of scope—a measure that shows functionality delivered.
- Having such a measure is a good practice as it provides information about whether an investment delivered the functionality that was paid for.
- In 2007, we recommended that IRS develop a quantitative measure of scope for BSM in order to have complete information on the performance of these investments.[1] IRS agreed with the recommendation, and in response, developed a measure to include in the fiscal year 2012 BSM expenditure plan. The agency, however, did not use the measure since the expenditure plan was discontinued.
  - IRS has several methods for ensuring that intended functionality is delivered, including project health assessment reports, which provide project status updates and flag risks; and end of test completion reports, which are signed off at the end of the development and deployment phases. None of these methods, however, provides for a quantitative measure of functionality delivered. Officials stated they recognize the value of developing such a measure and plan to determine a schedule for doing this.
- Until it develops a quantitative measure of scope (i.e., functionality delivered), IRS will not have complete information on the performance of its investments and will therefore have less assurance that it is effectively managing these investments.

[1]GAO, *Business Systems Modernization: Internal Revenue Service s Fiscal Year 2007 Expenditure Plan*, GAO-07-247 (Washington, D.C.: February 15, 2007).

Page 34

Legislative Proposals

GAO Has Conducted Analyses Related to 6 of 22 Legislative Proposals Included in the Budget Request for IRS

- The 22 legislative proposals are estimated to generate more than $12 billion over 10 years and are estimated to cost $80.2 million over 3 years.

Table 9: Legislative Proposals Related to Prior GAO Work (in millions)

IRS legislative proposals related to prior GAO work	Projected revenues over 10 years	Projected costs over 3 years	Related GAO reports
Increase certainty about the rules pertaining to classification of employees as independent contractors	$8,372	$1.9	GAO-09-717
Extend IRS math error authority in certain circumstances	$173	Not available	GAO-10-349, GAO-10-225
Allow IRS to absorb credit and debit card processing fees for certain tax payments	$19	$9.6	GAO-10-11
Improve and make permanent the provision authorizing the IRS to disclose certain return information to certain prison officials	Negligible revenue effect	Not available	GAO-06-100
Provide Treasury with the regulatory authority to require electronic filing of all Form 5500 Annual Report information	No revenue effect	$11.2	GAO-05-491
Require taxpayers who prepare their returns electronically, but file their returns on paper, to print their returns with a two-dimensional bar code	No revenue effect	$6.8	GAO-12-33, GAO-08-38

Sources: RS, Fiscal Year 2013 Congressional Budget Justification, and Department of the Treasury, *General Explanations of the Administration s Fiscal Year 2013 Revenue Proposals* (Washington, D.C.: February 2012).

Page 35

GAO Open Matters and Recommendations

IRS At Least Partially Implemented 5 Prior GAO Recommendations to Improve the Budget Presentation

Table 10. IRS Took Steps to Implement Prior Recommendations

Recommendations	Actions taken by IRS	Benefit
Extend the use of ROI in future budget proposals to include major enforcement programs.[a]	RS made a significant step forward in beginning to calculate actual ROIs for major enforcement programs. Specifically, RS captured actual revenue and cost associated for Exam, Collections and Automated Underreporter (AUR) programs. RS officials said they plan to report this data in the budget justification next year, pending various approvals.	Actual ROIs could provide information about how programs and initiatives are performing, and could serve as a basis for assessing the revenue and cost impact of program-level changes.
Develop ROIs for RS's enforcement programs using actual revenue and full cost data and compare the actual ROIs to the projected ROIs included in the full budget request.[b]	Although not at the program initiative level, RS made a significant step forward in beginning to calculate actual ROIs for major enforcement programs. Specifically, IRS captured actual revenues and costs associated for Exam, Collections and AUR programs. RS officials said they plan to report this data in the budget justification next year, pending various approvals.	Actual ROIs could provide information about how programs and initiatives are performing, and could serve as a basis for assessing the revenue and cost impact of program-level changes.
Report how savings beyond projections were used. The amount of explanation provided should correspond to the amount of savings.[c]	RS reported in the fiscal year 2013 budget request, how savings beyond projections were used. For fiscal year 2011, IRS reported that it realized $277.2 million and 960 FTE in actual savings—$86.5 million and 488 FTE more than projected.	Knowing how an agency spent excess savings, particularly in years when the excess is significant, could help Congress assess budgetary needs in the future.
Provide cost estimates for individual legislative proposals in future budget justifications.[c]	RS provided cost estimates for individual legislative proposals in the Fiscal Year 2013 Congressional Budget Justification for IRS.	By knowing estimated costs to implement an individual legislative proposal, Congress has important information to use when weighing proposals.
Include measures of cost and schedule performance for major IT systems in Operations Support, such as it does for BSM.[c]	RS included measures of cost and schedule performance for major IT systems in the Fiscal Year 2013 Congressional Budget Justification for IRS.	Congressional stakeholders we met with stated that having a summary of cost and scheduled performance for major IT systems in Operations Support would be helpful for oversight.

Source: GAO analysis.

[a]GAO-08-567

[b]GAO, *Internal Revenue Service: Review of the Fiscal Year 2010 Budget Request*, GAO-09-754 (Washington, D.C.: June 3, 2009).

[c]GAO-11-547

Page 36

GAO Open Matters and Recommendations

Some Prior Recommendations to Improve the Budget Presentation Remain Open

- Implementing the following recommendations could provide important information for budget decision makers.

Table 11: Some Recommendations to IRS Remain Open

Open recommendations	Benefit
Provide additional information, which could be qualitative if necessary to avoid losing existing reprogramming flexibility, about the program activities in the budget justification to better indicate RS's priorities.[a]	Program-level information increases Congress's ability to understand priorities and make more informed decisions about the use of resources.
Make explicit linkages between initiatives and proposals in the budget and strategic documents.[a]	Without an explicit and transparent connection between RS's strategic documents and the budget request, Congress and other stakeholders may not be able to understand the priority that IRS is giving to its efforts to improve service and enforcement.
Explain in the budget justification noteworthy changes in performance goals that reflect changes from previous performance and describe the impact on funding.[a]	Clear linkages between performance goals and funding can help determine how funded activities contribute to operational goals and specific measures. These linkages can also illustrate how targets align with funding and how efficiently resources are used.
Expand efforts to systematically identify savings and efficiencies as part of its budget development process on a periodic, but not necessarily annual, basis.[b]	Best practices suggest that agencies routinely identify savings and efficiencies. By not applying the more systematic and productive IT approach agency wide, RS might be missing opportunities to realize savings and efficiencies.

Source: GAO analysis of prior budget related reports.
[a] GAO-10-687R
[b] GAO-11-547

Page 37

GAO Open Matters and Recommendations

106 Open Matters for Congress and Recommendations to IRS Regarding Tax Administration Could Result in Potential Savings or Increased Revenues

- As of March 19, 2012, 33 GAO products contain 10 matters for Congress and 96 recommendations to IRS (see appendix VI).

- 32 increase revenue, 7 increase savings, 16 increase both savings and revenue, and 51 have indirect financial benefits. For example:
  - If Congress amended the Internal Revenue Code to make all taxpayers with rental real estate activity subject to the same information reporting requirements as other taxpayers operating a trade or business, IRS could generate $2.5 billion over 10 years.[a]
  - If IRS could obtain more helpful information about taxpayers' mortgages by expanding information collected on Form 1098, it could improve taxpayer compliance with statutory requirements and increase revenues.[b]

- Since last year, 1 matter and 25 recommendations were implemented.

[a]Joint Committee on Taxation, "Estimated Budget Effects of the Revenue Provisions Contained in the President's Fiscal Year 2011 Budget Proposal," JCX-7-10 R (March 15, 2010). [b]GAO, Home Mortgage Interest Deduction: Despite Challenges Presented by Complex Tax Rules, IRS Could Enhance Enforcement and Guidance, GAO-09-769 (Washington, D.C.: July 29, 2009).

Page 38

Conclusions

- We have identified several areas where budget decision makers lack information that would be helpful in making decisions about resource trade-offs at IRS.

  - Unlike most enforcement initiatives that IRS now justifies with ROI estimates, non-enforcement investment initiatives are not justified with similar economic analyses, such as cost-effectiveness analyses. When comparisons of alternative investments for accomplishing a goal do not consider costs, budget decision makers cannot be assured that alternatives were fully evaluated and that the best alternative was selected.
  - Without a timely, updated cost estimate for PPACA, budget decision makers will not know the fraction of the multi-year effort being funded in fiscal year 2013 or the subsequent remaining costs.
  - Because the budget request for hiring new staff is not based on expected hiring dates, but instead assumes hiring will occur at the beginning of the fiscal year, some funds will be available for other uses, which are not described or substantiated in the budget request.
  - Although IRS tracks the schedule and cost performance of IT investments, it does not have a quantitative measure to determine whether it is delivering planned functionality. Without this measure, budget decision makers lack complete information about IRS's performance in managing IT investment projects.

Page 39

Recommendations for Executive Action

- To continue to improve information on program cost and results that could aid in resource decision making, we recommend that the Commissioner of Internal Revenue

    - ensure cost-effectiveness analyses are conducted for future significant investments when there are alternative approaches for achieving a given benefit, such as for any new significant PPACA projects;

    - ensure that an updated PPACA cost estimate is completed by September 2012 in accordance with best practices in the GAO *Cost Guide*;

    - prepare funding requests for new staff based on estimated hiring dates; and

    - develop a quantitative measure of scope, at a minimum for its major IT investments, to have more complete information on the performance of these investments.

Page 40

Appendix II: Comments from the Internal Revenue Service

IRS Position Regarding GAO draft report dated May 17, 2012

IRS 2013 Budget: Continuing to Improve Information on Program Costs and Results Could Aid in Resource Decision Making (GAO-12-606).

The IRS appreciates the opportunity to review the draft GAO report regarding the IRS's FY 2013 President's Budget Submission. As in prior years, our budget submission reflects the continued improvement of the availability of information on program costs and the tools we use to support budget initiatives such as Return on Investment (ROI) calculations for both immediate and directly measurable revenue, as well as long term revenue effects for initiatives that do no have an immediate measurable ROI. The IRS provides the below Agency Position in regard to a few of the other areas addressed in the draft report:

Implementation of the Patient Protection Affordable Care Act (PPACA): The IRS agrees with the recommendations as they relate to implementing new investments, such as the those associated with PPACA and to ensuring that an updated PPACA cost estimate is completed by September 2012; however notes that the report does not acknowledge that although the FY 2013 request includes new funding for IRS appropriations, the majority of the funding supports on-going efforts and for staff already on board in FY 2012.

Development of a Quantitative Measure of Scope
While the IRS agrees with the recommendation to develop a quantitative measure of scope to present information on the performance of its major investments, the collective use of methods currently in place to document delivered functionality throughout the lifecycle. These methods include the use of business cases and valid reliable cost estimates which define the scope and value attributed to the investment. The progress of the investment is tracked through internal governance entities within the IT organization and additionally with business counterparts in Executive Steering Committees. Further more, project assessments are used to provide status updates in internal tracking systems to reflect the health of the project and flag any risks. Risks and supporting mitigations are also tracked to completion and escalated as necessary. As requirements are solidified, they are also tracked to ensure they meet functionality as intended. Finally, end of test completion reports provide the documentation for the desired end state and are signed off on as part of the Milestone exit at 4b & 5.

Development of Funding Requests for New Hires
While the IRS agrees with three of the four recommendations, as previously discussed with GAO, the IRS does not agree with the recommendation related to the development of funding requests for new staff based on estimated hiring dates and is concerned with the long term impact of such a recommendation. Not only is the current practice approved by OMB, but as in prior years, the IRS is committed to continuing to demonstrate full transparency in spending through the submission of the annual Operating Plan and requests for reprogramming that reflect any variance in spending as the result of late enactment of the budget or delayed hiring of new staff.

Appendix III: Reliability of Patient Protection and Affordable Care Act Cost Estimate

The following figures outline our assessment of the extent to which the Internal Revenue Service's (IRS) Fiscal Year 2013 Patient Protection and Affordable Care Act (PPACA) cost estimate for new initiatives meet best practices. This information is repeated in table 1, following the graphics.

Figure 1: How IRS's Fiscal Year 2013 PPACA Cost Estimate Aligns with the Best Practices for Comprehensiveness

Directions:

Rollover each below to see further information on cost estimation best practices.

Overall assessment:

Partially meets best practices for a comprehensive cost estimate.

A comprehensive cost estimate:

Best practices characteristics		Assessment of whether best practices are met	Effect
Includes all life-cycle costs.		The Modernization and Information Technology Services (MITS) cost estimate contains all the IT needs for the program as known at the time of the estimate. The MITS estimate cost model includes labor and non labor costs as well as government and contractor costs, but they are only included for fiscal year 2010 through fiscal year 2013. Investment and operations and maintenance costs are included only for the same time period. The cost model did not mention disposal costs. Partially meets	A life–cycle cost estimate should encompass all past (or sunk), present, and future costs for every aspect of the program, regardless of funding source, including all government and contractor costs. Without fully accounting for life-cycle costs, management will have difficulty successfully planning program resource requirements and making wise decisions.
Completely defines the program, reflects the current schedule, and is technically reasonable.		The cost model documentation only discusses the architecture and project timeline, which is just part of the technical description. Partially meets	Understanding the program—including the acquisition strategy, technical definition, characteristics, system design features, and technologies to be included—is key to developing a credible cost estimate. Without these data, the cost estimator will not be able to identify the technical and program parameters that will bind the cost estimate.
Has a product-oriented work breakdown structure (WBS), traceable to the program's technical scope at an appropriate level of detail.		The WBS has not been modified since our 2011 review[a] and does not include a schedule or EVM reporting. It is still based on high level requirements and is not standardized. However, a WBS and dictionary are now part of the statement of work for the cost estimate. Partially meets	Without a WBS, the program lacks a framework to develop a schedule and cost plan that can easily track technical accomplishments—in terms of resources spent in relation to the plan as well as completion of activities and tasks.
Documents all cost-influencing ground rules and assumptions.		Ground rules and assumptions are defined for each cost element in the cost model spreadsheet, assigned according to WBS, and reflect relevant historical data. However, we found no evidence that the assumptions were associated with any risk analysis or developed with input from IRS's technical community or were approved by management. The effect of budget constraints has not been identified despite the fact that the program has already experienced budget cuts. Partially meets	Unless ground rules and assumptions are clearly documented, the cost estimate will not have a basis for resolving potential risks. Furthermore, the estimate cannot be reconstructed when the original estimators are no longer available.

Source: GAO analysis of IRS's Fiscal Year 2013 PPACA cost estimate and GAO-09-3SP.

Note: We determined the overall assessment rating by assigning the following ratings: Partially Meets – IRS provided evidence that satisfies about half of the criterion.

[a]GAO, *Patient Protection and Affordable Care Act: IRS Should Expand Its Strategic Approach to Implementation*, GAO-11-719 (Washington, D.C.: June 29, 2011).

Figure 2: How IRS's Fiscal Year 2013 PPACA Cost Estimate Aligns with the Best Practices for Being Well Documented

Directions:

Rollover each below to see further information on cost estimation best practices.

Overall assessment:

Partially meets best practices for a well documented cost estimate.

A well documented cost estimate should:

Best practices characteristics		Assessment of whether best practices are met	Effect
Capture the source data used, the reliability of the data, and how the data were made compatible with other data in the estimate.		Only some sources of data are shown in cost model. The cost estimate does not address the reliability of the data or if historical data was made compatible with other data in the estimate. Partially meets	Data are the foundation of every cost estimate. The quality of the data affects the estimate's overall credibility. Depending on the data quality, an estimate can range anywhere from a mere guess to a highly defensible cost position. However, without sufficient background knowledge about the source and reliability of the data, the cost estimator cannot know with any confidence whether the data collected can be used directly or need to be modified.
Describe the calculations and the methodology used to derive each element's cost.		Calculations are shown in a spreadsheet cost model. However, some of the estimates were based on expert opinion with no historical data provided to back up the estimates. Substantially meets	(a)
Describe how the estimate was developed.		Step by step calculations are shown. However, as mentioned above there were several subprojects that had cost estimates based on expert opinion that were hard coded into the cost model, which makes it difficult to understand how these estimates were developed. Substantially meets	(a)
Discuss the technical baseline description.		The cost model documentation only discusses some of the technical baseline description. Partially meets	Without a technical baseline, the cost estimate will not be based on a comprehensive program description and will lack specific information regarding technical and program risks.
Provide evidence of management review and acceptance.		Program officials said approval of the cost estimate was given by the Commissioner's Office. However, documentation showing management acceptance of the cost estimate was not provided. Minimally meets	A cost estimate is not considered valid until management has approved it. It is imperative that management understand how the estimate was developed, including the risks associated with the underlying data and methods.

Source: GAO analysis of IRS's Fiscal Year 2013 PPACA cost estimate and GAO-09-3SP.

Note: We determined the overall assessment rating by assigning the following ratings: Minimally Meets – IRS provided evidence that satisfies a small portion of the criterion, Partially Meets – IRS provided evidence that satisfies about half of the criterion, Substantially Meets – IRS provided evidence that satisfies a large portion of the criterion.

aWe did not describe effects for characteristics scored as "substantially meets."

Figure 3: How IRS's Fiscal Year 2013 PPACA Cost Estimate Aligns with the Best Practices For Accuracy

Directions:

Rollover each below to see further information on cost estimation best practices.

Overall assessment:

Partially meets best practices for an accurate cost estimate.

An accurate cost estimate:

Best practices characteristics		Assessment of whether best practices are met	Effect
Produces unbiased results.		The cost estimate budget was based on a high estimate as the program is in a very early stage and a lot of uncertainty remains. According to IRS officials, there is a 60 to 70 percent confidence rate that the estimate will fall between the low and high range of cost. Partially meets	A cost estimate is biased if the estimated work is overly conservative or too optimistic. Unless the estimate is based on an assessment of the most likely costs and reflects the degree of uncertainty given all of the risks considered, management will not be able to make informed decisions.
Is properly adjusted for inflation.		Inflation was not used in the cost model. Does not meet	Adjusting for inflation is important because in the development of an estimate, cost data must be expressed in like terms. If a mistake is made or the inflation amount is not correct, cost overruns can result.
Contains few mistakes.		IRS did a line by line check of the estimate to validate it. We also performed a check of the spreadsheets provided and found no errors. Fully meets	(a)
Is regularly updated to reflect significant program changes.		The IT cost estimate has not been updated since October 2010, except that IRS did include actual costs for fiscal year 2011. Further, documentation did not show that staffing estimates were re-evaluated for fiscal year 2013. However, on April 26, 2012 IRS awarded a contract to update the entire development cost estimate which includes both the IT and staffing portions. Minimally meets	If a cost estimate is not updated, it can become more difficult to analyze changes in program costs and collecting cost and technical data to support future estimates will be hindered. Cost estimates not updated when the technical baseline changes will lack credibility.
Documents and explains variances between planned and actual costs.		Actual costs are being tracked, but the documentation does not discuss variances or lessons learned. Minimally meets	Without a documented comparison between the current estimate (updated with actual costs) and the old estimate, cost estimators cannot determine the level of variance between the two estimates. That is, the estimators cannot see how well they are estimating and how the program is changing over time.
Reflects cost estimating experiences from comparable programs.		The majority of the estimate was based on historical data. Substantially meets	(a)

Source: GAO analysis of IRS's Fiscal Year 2013 PPACA cost estimate and GAO-09-3SP.

Note: We determined the overall assessment rating by assigning the following ratings: Does Not Meet – IRS provided no evidence that satisfies any of the criterion, Minimally Meets – IRS provided evidence that satisfies a small portion of the criterion, Partially Meets – IRS provided evidence that satisfies about half of the criterion, Substantially Meets – IRS provided evidence that satisfies a large portion of the criterion, Fully Meets – IRS provided complete evidence that satisfies the entire criterion.

[a]We did not describe effects for characteristics scored as "fully meets" or "substantially meets."

Figure 4: How IRS's Fiscal Year 2013 PPACA Cost Estimate Aligns with the Best Practices for Credibility

| Directions:

| Rollover each below to see further information on cost estimation best practices.

Overall assessment:

Minimally meets best practices for a credible cost estimate.

A credible cost estimate includes:

Best practices characteristics	Assessment of whether best practices are met	Effect
A sensitivity analysis that identifies a range of possible costs based on varying inputs.	Each element of the cost estimate is presented as a high, low, and most likely range of costs. However, it is not clear how each changing each variable would affect the overall total cost. Minimally meets	Without sensitivity analysis that reveals how the cost estimate is affected by a change in a single assumption, the cost estimator will not fully understand which variable most affects the cost estimate.
A risk and uncertainty analysis.	Each element of the cost estimate is presented with a high, low, and most likely range of costs. However, a comprehensive risk and uncertainty analysis was not completed. The program has already experienced a reduced budget in fiscal year 2012. The IRS requested $473 million, but the request was not funded, so IRS revised its fiscal year 2012 spending plan to $332.2 million from HHS funds. However, the IRS has not considered the risk of future budget reductions on the estimate. By not risk adjusting the estimate, the IRS risks either running behind schedule or incurring more costs to maintain the schedule. Minimally meets	For management to make good decisions, the program estimate must reflect the degree of uncertainty, so that a level of confidence can be given about the estimate. Having a range of costs around a point estimate is more useful to decision makers because it conveys the level of confidence in achieving the most likely cost and also informs them on cost, schedule, and technical risks.
Cross-checking of major cost elements.	No evidence of any cross-checks was found in the cost estimate documentation. Does not meet	One way to reinforce the credibility of the cost estimate is to see whether applying a different method produces similar results. The main purpose of cross-checking is to determine whether alternative methods produce similar results. If so, then confidence in the estimate increases, leading to greater credibility.
A comparison to an in-dependent cost estimate conducted by another organization.	On April 26, 2012, IRS awarded a contract to update the PPACA cost estimate. The contract was provided and closely matches the best practices of the GAO cost guide. IRS officials told us they plan to use the IRS Estimation Program Office (EPO) to perform validation of the revised cost estimate from the contractor. Having the EPO create an independent cost estimate to validate the hired cost estimating contractor will provide assurance that the delivered cost estimate is high quality. Minimally meets	A program estimate that has not been reconciled with an independent cost estimate has an increased risk of proceeding underfunded because an independent cost estimate provides an objective and unbiased assessment of whether the program estimate can be achieved.

Source: GAO analysis of IRS's Fiscal Year 2013 PPACA cost estimate and GAO-09-3SP.

Note: We determined the overall assessment rating by assigning the following ratings: Does Not Meet – IRS provided no evidence that satisfies any of the criterion, Minimally Meets – IRS provided evidence that satisfies a small portion of the criterion.

The following table outlines our assessment of the extent to which IRS's Fiscal Year 2013 PPACA cost estimate for new initiatives meet best practices. This information is also depicted in the previous figures 1-4.

Table 1: How IRS's Fiscal Year 2013 PPACA Cost Estimate Aligns with Best Practices Outlined in the GAO Cost Guide

Best practices characteristics	Overall assessment	Assessment of whether best practices are met	Effect
A **comprehensive** cost estimate:	Partially meets best practices for a comprehensive cost estimate		
Includes all life-cycle costs. A life-cycle cost estimate provides a complete and structured accounting of all resources and associated cost elements required to develop, produce, deploy, and sustain a particular program. It should cover the inception of the program through its retirement.		The Modernization and Information Technology Services (MITS) cost estimate contains all the IT needs for the program as known at the time of the estimate. The MITS estimate cost model includes labor and non labor costs as well as government and contractor costs, but they are only included for fiscal year 2010 through fiscal year 2013. Investment and operations and maintenance costs are included only for the same time period. The cost model did not mention disposal costs. (*Partially meets.*)	A life-cycle cost estimate should encompass all past (or sunk), present, and future costs for every aspect of the program, regardless of funding source, including all government and contractor costs. Without fully accounting for life-cycle costs, management will have difficulty successfully planning program resource requirements and making wise decisions.
Completely defines the program, reflects the current schedule, and is technically reasonable. The cost estimate should be based on a documented technical baseline description, which provides a common definition of the program, including detailed technical, program, and schedule descriptions of the system.		The cost model documentation only discusses the architecture and project timeline, which is just part of the technical description. (*Partially meets.*)	Understanding the program—including the acquisition strategy, technical definition, characteristics, system design features, and technologies to be included—is key to developing a credible cost estimate. Without these data, the cost estimator will not be able to identify the technical and program parameters that will bind the cost estimate.

Best practices characteristics	Overall assessment	Assessment of whether best practices are met	Effect
Has a product-oriented work breakdown structure (WBS), traceable to the program's technical scope at an appropriate level of detail. A WBS provides a basic framework for a variety of related activities like estimating costs, developing schedules, identifying resources and potential risks, and providing the means for measuring program status using earned value management (EVM). It is product-oriented if it allows a program to track cost and schedule by defined deliverables, such as a hardware or software component.		The WBS has not been modified since our 2011 review[a] and does not include a schedule or EVM reporting. It is still based on high level requirements and is not standardized. However, a WBS and dictionary are now part of the statement of work for the upcoming new cost estimate. (*Partially meets*.)	Without a WBS, the program lacks a framework to develop a schedule and cost plan that can easily track technical accomplishments—in terms of resources spent in relation to the plan as well as completion of activities and tasks.
Documents all cost-influencing ground rules and assumptions. Cost estimates are typically based on limited information and therefore need to be bound by ground rules and assumptions. Ground rules are a set of estimating standards that provide guidance and common definitions, while assumptions are judgments about past, present, or future conditions that may affect the estimate. Any risks associated with assumptions should be identified and traced to specific WBS elements.		Ground rules and assumptions are defined for each cost element in the cost model spreadsheet, assigned according to WBS, and reflect relevant historical data. However, we found no evidence that the assumptions were associated with any risk analysis or developed with input from IRS's technical community or were approved by management. The effect of budget constraints has not been identified despite the fact that the program has already experienced budget cuts. (*Partially meets*.)	Unless ground rules and assumptions are clearly documented, the cost estimate will not have a basis for resolving potential risks. Furthermore, the estimate cannot be reconstructed when the original estimators are no longer available.
A **well documented** cost estimate should:	Partially meets best practices for a well documented cost estimate.		

Best practices characteristics	Overall assessment	Assessment of whether best practices are met	Effect
Capture the source data used, the reliability of the data, and how the data were made compatible with other data in the estimate. Data should be collected from primary sources. The source, content, time, and units should be adequately documented. Further, data should be analyzed to determine accuracy and reliability, and to identify cost drivers.		Only some sources of data are shown in cost model. The cost estimate does not address the reliability of the data or if historical data was made compatible with other data in the estimate. (*Partially meets.*)	Data are the foundation of every cost estimate. The quality of the data affects the estimate's overall credibility. Depending on the data quality, an estimate can range anywhere from a mere guess to a highly defensible cost position. However, without sufficient background knowledge about the source and reliability of the data, the cost estimator cannot know with any confidence whether the data collected can be used directly or need to be modified.
Describe the calculations and the methodology used to derive each element's cost. Documentation should describe what calculation methods are used, as well as how they were applied, and explain any anomalies.		Calculations are shown in a spreadsheet cost model. However, some of the estimates were based on expert opinion with no historical data provided to back up the estimates. (*Substantially meets.*)	(^{b})
Describe how the estimate was developed. The data supporting the estimate should be available and adequately documented so that the estimate can be easily updated to reflect actual costs or program changes.		Step by step calculations are shown. However, as mentioned above there were several subprojects that had cost estimates based on expert opinion that were hard coded into the cost model, which makes it difficult to understand how these estimates were developed. (*Substantially meets.*)	(^{b})
Discuss the technical baseline description. A technical baseline description provides a common definition of the program, including detailed technical, program, and schedule descriptions of the system, for a cost estimate to be built on. The data in the technical baseline should be consistent with the cost estimate.		The cost model documentation only discusses some of the technical baseline description. (*Partially meets.*)	Without a technical baseline, the cost estimate will not be based on a comprehensive program description and will lack specific information regarding technical and program risks.

Best practices characteristics	Overall assessment	Assessment of whether best practices are met	Effect
Provide evidence of management review and acceptance. There should be a briefing to management, including a clear explanation of how the cost estimate was derived. Management's acceptance of the cost estimate should be documented.		Program officials said approval of the cost estimate was given by the Commissioner's Office. However, documentation showing management acceptance of the cost estimate was not provided. (*Minimally meets.*)	A cost estimate is not considered valid until management has approved it. It is imperative that management understand how the estimate was developed, including the risks associated with the underlying data and methods.
An **accurate** cost estimate:	*Partially meets* best practices for an accurate cost estimate.		
Produces unbiased results. Cost estimates should have an uncertainty analysis, which determines where the estimate falls against the range of all possible costs.		The cost estimate budget was based on a high estimate as the program is in a very early stage and a lot of uncertainty remains. According to IRS officials, there is a 60 to 70 percent confidence rate that the estimate will fall between the low and high range of cost. (*Partially meets.*)	A cost estimate is biased if the estimated work is overly conservative or too optimistic. Unless the estimate is based on an assessment of the most likely costs and reflects the degree of uncertainty given all of the risks considered, management will not be able to make informed decisions.
Is properly adjusted for inflation. Cost data should be adjusted for inflation to ensure that comparisons and projections are valid. Data should also be normalized to constant year dollars to remove the effects of inflation. Also, inflation assumptions must be well documented.		Inflation was not used in the cost model. (*Does not meet.*)	Adjusting for inflation is important because in the development of an estimate, cost data must be expressed in like terms. If a mistake is made or the inflation amount is not correct, cost overruns can result.
Contains few mistakes. Results should be checked for accuracy, double counting, and omissions. Validating that a cost estimate is accurate requires thoroughly understanding and investigating how the cost model was constructed.		IRS did a line by line check of the estimate to validate it. We also performed a check of the spreadsheets provided and found no errors. (*Fully meets.*)	([b])

Best practices characteristics	Overall assessment	Assessment of whether best practices are met	Effect
Is regularly updated to reflect significant program changes. The cost estimate should be updated to reflect significant program changes, such as changes to schedules or other assumptions. Updates should also reflect actual costs so that the estimate always reflects the current program status.		The IT cost estimate has not been updated since October 2010, except that IRS did include actual costs for 2011. Further, documentation did not show that staffing estimates were re-evaluated for fiscal year 2013. However, on April 26, 2012 IRS awarded a contract to update the entire development cost estimate which includes both the IT and staffing portions. (*Minimally meets.*)	If a cost estimate is not updated, it can become more difficult to analyze changes in program costs and collecting cost and technical data to support future estimates will be hindered. Cost estimates not updated when the technical baseline changes will lack credibility.
Documents and explains variances between planned and actual costs. Variances between planned and actual costs should be documented, explained, and reviewed. For any elements whose actual costs or schedules differ from the estimate, the estimate should discuss variances and lessons learned.		Actual costs are being tracked but the documentation does not discuss variances or lessons learned. (*Minimally meets.*)	Without a documented comparison between the current estimate (updated with actual costs) and the old estimate, cost estimators cannot determine the level of variance between the two estimates. That is, the estimators cannot see how well they are estimating and how the program is changing over time.
Reflects cost estimating experiences from comparable programs. The estimate should be based on historical cost estimation data and actual experiences from other comparable programs. These data should be reliable and relevant to the new program.		The majority of the estimate was based on historical data. (*Substantially meets.*)	([b])
A **credible** cost estimate includes:	Minimally meets best practices for a credible cost estimate.		

Best practices characteristics	Overall assessment	Assessment of whether best practices are met	Effect
A sensitivity analysis that identifies a range of possible costs based on varying inputs. A sensitivity analysis examines how changes to key assumptions and inputs affect the estimate. The estimate should identify key cost drivers, examine their parameters and assumptions, and re-estimate the total cost by varying each parameter between its minimum and maximum range.		Each element of the cost estimate is presented as a high, low, and most likely range of costs. However, it is not clear how changing each variable would affect the overall total cost. (*Minimally meets.*)	Without sensitivity analysis that reveals how the cost estimate is affected by a change in a single assumption, the cost estimator will not fully understand which variable most affects the cost estimate.
A risk and uncertainty analysis. A risk and uncertainty analysis recognizes the potential for error and attempts to quantify it by identifying the effects of changing key cost drivers.		Each element of the cost estimate is presented with a high, low, and most likely range of costs. However, a comprehensive risk and uncertainty analysis was not completed. The program has already experienced a reduced budget in fiscal year 2012. The IRS requested $473 million, but the request was not funded so IRS revised its fiscal year 2012 spending plan to $332.2 million from HHS funds. However, the IRS has not considered the risk of future budget reductions on the estimate. By not risk adjusting the estimate, the IRS risks either running behind schedule or incurring more costs to maintain the schedule. (*Minimally meets.*)	For management to make good decisions, the program estimate must reflect the degree of uncertainty, so that a level of confidence can be given about the estimate. Having a range of costs around a point estimate is more useful to decision makers because it conveys the level of confidence in achieving the most likely cost and also informs them on cost, schedule, and technical risks.
Cross-checking of major cost elements. A cross-check is done by using a different cost estimation method to see if it produces similar results.		No evidence of any cross-checks was found in the cost estimate documentation. (*Does not meet.*)	One way to reinforce the credibility of the cost estimate is to see whether applying a different method produces similar results. The main purpose of cross-checking is to determine whether alternative methods produce similar results. If so, then confidence in the estimate increases, leading to greater credibility.

Best practices characteristics	Overall assessment	Assessment of whether best practices are met	Effect
A comparison to an independent cost estimate conducted by another organization. A second, independent cost estimate should be performed by an organization outside of the program office's influence. It should be based on the same technical baseline, ground rules, and assumptions as the original estimate.		IRS awarded a contract to update the PPACA cost estimate on April 26, 2012. The statement of work for this contract was provided and closely matches the best practices of the GAO *Cost Guide*. IRS officials told us they plan to use the IRS Estimation Program Office (EPO) to perform validation of the revised cost estimate from the contractor. Having the EPO create an independent cost estimate to validate the hired cost estimating contractor will provide assurance that the delivered cost estimate is high quality. (*Minimally meets*.)	A program estimate that has not been reconciled with an independent cost estimate has an increased risk of proceeding underfunded because an independent cost estimate provides an objective and unbiased assessment of whether the program estimate can be achieved.

Source: GAO analysis of IRS's Fiscal Year 2013 PPACA cost estimate and GAO-09-3SP.

Note: We determined the overall assessment rating by assigning the following ratings: Does Not Meet–IRS provided no evidence that satisfies any of the criterion, Minimally Meets–IRS provided evidence that satisfies a small portion of the criterion, Partially Meets–IRS provided evidence that satisfies about half of the criterion, Substantially Meets–IRS provided evidence that satisfies a large portion of the criterion, Fully Meets–IRS provided complete evidence that satisfies the entire criterion.

[a]GAO, *Patient Protection and Affordable Care Act: IRS Should Expand Its Strategic Approach to Implementation,* GAO-11-719 (Washington, D.C.: June 29, 2011).

[b]We did not descrbe effects for characteristics scored as "fully meets" or "substantially meets."

Appendix IV: Description of the Internal Revenue Service's Major Information Technology Investments

Table 2: The Internal Revenue Service's 20 Major Information Technology Investments

Investment Name	Investment Description
Account Management Services (AMS)	This investment is intended to enhance customer support by providing applications that enable IRS employees to access, validate, and update individual taxpayer accounts on demand.
Affordable Care Act (ACA) Administration[a]	This investment allows the IRS to continue the development of new systems and modification of existing systems required to support new tax credits as prescribed in the Affordable Care Act.
Current Customer Account Data Engine (CADE)	This investment was intended to deploy a modernized database foundation that would replace the IRS's Individual Master File processing system and house tax information for more than 200 million taxpayers while providing faster return processing and refunds. According to IRS, the Current CADE Investment ended on December 31, 2011.
CADE 2	This investment is intended to leverage knowledge gained from the development on Current CADE and data from the Individual Master File to provide timely access to authoritative individual taxpayer account information and also enhance IRS's ability to address technology, security, financial material weaknesses, and long-term architectural planning and viability.
Electronic Fraud Detection System (EFDS)	This investment is intended to detect fraud at the time that tax returns are filed in order to eliminate the issuance of fraudulent tax refunds.
e-Services (e-SVS)	This investment is several web-based self-assisted services that are intended to allow authorized individuals to do business with the IRS electronically.
Foreign Account Tax Compliance Act (FATCA)	This investment requires foreign financial institutions to report to the IRS information about financial accounts held by U.S. taxpayers, or foreign entities in which U.S. taxpayers hold a substantial ownership interest as required by the FATCA.
Implement Return Review Program (RRP; replaces EFDS)	This investment, currently under development, is intended to maximize fraud detection at the time that tax returns are filed to eliminate issuance of questionable refunds.
Individual Master File (IMF)	This investment is the authoritative data source for individual tax account data. All other IRS information systems that process IMF data depend on output from this source. This investment is a critical component of IRS's ability to process tax returns.
Information Reporting and Document Matching (IRDM)	This investment is intended to establish a new business information matching program in order to increase voluntary compliance and accurate income reporting.
Integrated Customer Communication Environment (ICCE)	This investment includes several projects that are intended to simplify voluntary compliance using voice response, Internet, and other computer technology such as the Modernized Internet Employee Identification Number (Mod IEIN), which allows third parties to act on the behalf of taxpayers.
Integrated Data Retrieval System (IDRS)	This investment is intended to provide systemic review, improve consistency in case control, alleviate staffing needs, issue notices to taxpayers, and allow taxpayers to see status of refunds. It is a mission-critical system used by 60,000 IRS employees.
Integrated Financial System/CORE Financial System (IFS)	This investment is the financial system used by IRS for budget, payroll, accounts payable/receivable, general ledger functions, and financial reporting. IRS uses this system to report on the cost of operations and to manage budgets by fiscal year.
Integrated Submission and Remittance Processing System (ISRP)	This investment is intended to process paper tax returns, and updates tax forms to comply with tax law changes.
IRS End User Systems and Services (EUSS)	This investment is intended to support products and services necessary for daily functions for over 100,000 IRS employees at headquarters and field sites.

Investment Name	Investment Description
IRS Main Frames and Servers Services and Support (MSSS)	This investment is intended to support the design, development and deployment of server storage infrastructures, software, databases, and operating systems.
IRS Telecommunications Systems and Support (TSS)	This investment supports IRS's broad and local network infrastructure such as servers, and switches for voice, data, and video servicing of about 1,000 IRS sites.
IRS.GOV - Portal Environment	This investment is intended to provide web-based services such as tax filing and refund tracking, to internal and external users, such as IRS employees and other government agencies, taxpayers, and business partners.
Modernized e-File (MeF)	This investment is intended to provide a secure web-based platform for electronic tax filing of individual and business tax and information returns by registered Electronic Return Originators.
Service Center Recognition/Image Processing System (SCRIPS)	This investment is intended to be a data capture, management, and image storage system using high-speed scanning and digital imaging to convert data from the 940, 941, K-1, and paper returns from Information Returns Processing, into electronic format.

Source: GAO analysis of IRS data.

Notes: According to IRS, major investments are defined by the Department of Treasury as those that cost $10 million in either current year or budget year, or $50 million over the 5 year period extending from the prior year through budget year +2.

[a]IRS is implementing the Patient Protection and Affordable Care Act requirements under the investment name of ACA.

GAO-12-603 IRS 2013 Budget

Appendix V: Major Information Technology Investments with Significant Cost and Schedule Variances

Of the 20 major Information Technology (IT) investments, 6 had significant variances from the planned cost or schedule estimates.[1] A significant variance is defined as 10 percent over or under the planned estimate.

Affordable Care Act

Table 3: Cost and Schedule Performance Information for Affordable Care Act Administration

Reporting months	Planned days	Projected/ actual days	Schedule variance (planned days– projected/ actual days)	Schedule variance (in percent)	Planned costs (in millions)	Actual costs (in millions)	Costs variance (planned costs–actual costs) (in millions)	Cost variance (in percent)
Quarter 1 2012	—[a]	—[a]	—[a]	—[a]	$27.84	$19.68	$8.16	29.31
Quarter 2 2012	—[a]	—[a]	—[a]	—[a]	95.40	72.89	22.51	23.60

Source: Internal Revenue Service data.

Note: Numbers may not add due to rounding.

[a]The Internal Revenue Service did not provide us with any data on planned or actual schedule for this investment, but reported that it did not experience any variance.

- The Internal Revenue Service (IRS) officials stated that Affordable Care Act (ACA) was about 29 percent under planned cost during the first quarter of 2012 due to hardware and software acquisitions that have been postponed until later in fiscal year 2012.[2]
- According to IRS officials, ACA was approximately 24 percent under planned costs during the second quarter of 2012 due to
  - lower than expected labor costs, and
  - a delay in the receipt of funding for this quarter.

---

[1]According to IRS, major investments are defined by the Department of Treasury as those that cost $10 million in either current year or budget year, or $50 million over the 5 year period extending from the prior year through budget year +2.

[2]IRS is implementing the Patient Protection and Affordable Care Act requirements under the investment name of ACA.

Current Customer Account Data Engine

Table 4: Cost and Schedule Performance Information for Current Customer Account Data Engine

Reporting months	Planned days	Projected/ actual days	Schedule variance (planned days –projected/ actual days)	Schedule variance (in percent)	Planned costs (in millions)	Projected costs (in millions)	Costs variance (planned costs– projected costs) (in millions)	Cost variance (in percent)
October 2011	549	549	0	0	$1.95	$1.95	0.00	0.00
November 2011	549	549	0	0	1.95	1.95	0.00	0.00
December 2011	549	549	0	0	1.95	1.95	0.00	0.00
January 2012	549	549	0	0	1.95	1.95	0.00	0.00
February 2012	549	549	0	0	1.95	2.68	-0.73	-37.48
March 2012	549	549	0	0	1.95	1.97	-0.03	-1.41[a]

Source: IRS data.

Note: Numbers may not add due to rounding.

[a]Variance under 10 percent is not considered significant.

- According to IRS officials, Current Customer Account Data Engine[3] (CADE) was significantly over planned costs in February 2012 due to the need for additional resources to help close down the system and redistribute hardware and software assets to other projects within the IRS.

---

[3]According to IRS, the Current CADE investment ended on December 31, 2011.

Integrated Customer Communications Environment

Table 5: Cost and Schedule Performance Information for Integrated Customer Communication Environment

Reporting months	Planned days	Projected/ actual days	Schedule variance (planned days –projected/ actual days)	Schedule variance (in percent)	Planned costs (in millions)	Projected costs (in millions)	Costs variance (planned costs– projected costs) (in millions)	Cost variance (in percent)
October 2011	303	303	0	0	$3.74	$3.74	0.00	0.00
November 2011	303	303	0	0	3.74	3.74	0.00	0.00
December 2011	303	303	0	0	3.74	2.76	0.98	26.16
January 2012	303	303	0	0	3.74	2.76	0.98	26.16
February 2012	303	303	0	0	3.74	2.76	0.98	26.16
March 2012	303	303	0	0	3.74	2.49	1.25	33.47

Source: IRS data.

Note: Numbers may not add due to rounding.

- According to IRS officials, although contractor costs were higher than originally estimated, spending on Integrated Customer Communication Environment (ICCE) was significantly less than originally planned between December 2011 and March 2012 because:

  - costs associated with Foreign Account Tax Compliance Act were removed as part of plans to create a new, separate investment for IRS, and
  - some indirect costs associated with the Federal Student Aid activity may not have been fully reported within the financial system.

Integrated Submission and Remittance Processing System

Table 6: Cost and Schedule Performance Information for Integrated Submission and Remittance Processing System

Reporting months	Planned days	Projected/ actual days	Schedule variance (planned days – projected/ actual days)	Schedule variance (in percent)	Planned costs (in millions)	Projected costs (in millions)	Costs variance (planned costs– projected costs) (in millions)	Cost variance (in percent)
October 2011	547	547	0	0	$0.27	$0.27	0.00	0.00
November 2011	547	547	0	0	0.27	0.27	0.00	0.00
December 2011	547	547	0	0	0.27	0.27	0.00	0.00
January 2012	547	547	0	0	0.27	0.27	0.00	0.00
February 2012	547	577	-30	-5.48[a]	0.27	0.27	0.00	1.11[a]
March 2012	547	577	-60	-10.97	0.27	0.27	0.00	1.11[a]

Source: IRS data.

Note: Numbers may not add due to rounding.

[a]Variance under 10 percent is not considered significant.

- According to IRS officials, Integrated Submission and Remittance Processing System (ISRP) was approximately 11 percent behind planned schedule as of March 2012. IRS officials stated that this variance was caused by delays in the programming requirements for two projects, which extended the projected completion date by 2 months.

IRS Main Frames and Servers Services and Support

Table 7: Cost and Schedule Performance Information for IRS Main Frames and Servers Services and Support

Reporting months	Planned days	Projected/ actual days	Schedule variance (planned days –projected/ actual days)	Schedule variance (in percent)	Planned costs (in millions)	Projected costs (in millions)	Costs variance (planned costs– projected costs) (in millions)	Cost variance (in percent)
October 2011	—[a]	—[a]	—[a]	—[a]	—[a]	—[a]	—[a]	—[a]
November 2011	—[a]	—[a]	—[a]	—[a]	—[a]	—[a]	—[a]	—[a]
December 2011	498	1056	-558	-112.05	$19.68	$19.68	0.00	0.00
January 2012	249	863	-614	-246.59	9.84	9.84	0.00	0.00
February 2012	249	863	-614	-246.59	9.84	9.84	0.00	0.00
March 2012	737	737	0	0	9.84	9.84	0.00	0.00

Source: IRS data.

Note: Numbers may not add due to rounding.

[a]IRS did not provide cost or schedule data for these months, but reported there were no cost or schedule issues.

- According to IRS officials, IRS Main Frames and Servers Services and Support (MSSS) was significantly behind planned schedule between December 2011 and February 2012. IRS officials stated that the delays were caused by several issues including:
  - the Storage Area Network (SAN) Switch Refresh project procurement process exceeding anticipated time frames, and
  - the Modernized Infrastructure Solaris 10 & Supporting Technologies Upgrade (MISSTU) project experienced resource conflicts and various technical issues.

Modernized e-File

Table 8: Cost and Schedule Performance Information for Modernized e-File

Reporting months	Planned days	Projected/ actual days	Schedule variance (planned days –projected/ actual days)	Schedule variance (in percent)	Planned costs (in millions)	Projected costs (in millions)	Costs variance (planned costs– projected costs) (in millions)	Cost variance (in percent)
October 2011	837	837	0	0	$62.03	$62.03	0.00	0.00
November 2011	837	837	0	0	62.03	67.83	-5.80	-9.35[a]
December 2011	837	837	0	0	62.03	67.83	-5.80	-9.35[a]
January 2012	837	837	0	0	62.03	67.83	-5.80	-9.35[a]
February 2012	837	837	0	0	62.03	68.47	-6.44	-10.39
March 2012	837	837	-61	-7.29[a]	62.03	73.67	-11.64	-18.77

Source: IRS data.

Note: Numbers may not add due to rounding.

[a]Variance under 10 percent is not considered significant.

- According to IRS, Modernized e-File (MeF) is approximately 19 percent over planned costs in February and March 2012 due to a number of unanticipated and unplanned work activities, such as, performance testing and the purchase of additional hardware and software.

Appendix VI: GAO Products with Open Matters for Congress and Recommendations to the IRS Regarding Tax Administration

Thirty-three GAO products contain 10 matters for Congress and 96 recommendations to the Internal Revenue Service (IRS). Thirty-two increase revenue, 7 increase savings, 16 increase both savings and revenue, and 51 have indirect financial benefits.

Table 9: List of Open Matters for Congress and Recommendations to IRS That Could Result In Potential Savings or Increased Revenues

Report title and number	Website for current status of matters and/or recommendations	Potential financial impact
Detecting abusive tax avoidance transactions		
Abusive Tax Avoidance Transactions: IRS Needs Better Data to Inform Decisions about Transactions (GAO-11-493)	http://www.gao.gov/products/GAO-11-493	IR, IFB
Enhancing budget requests		
IRS Budget 2012: Extending Systematic Reviews of Spending Could Identify More Savings Over Time (GAO-11-547)	http://www.gao.gov/products/GAO-11-547	IS
Enhancing collection of user fees		
User Fees: Additional Guidance and Documentation Could Further Strengthen IRS's Biennial Review of Fees (GAO-12-193)	http://www.gao.gov/products/GAO-12-193	IFB
Enhancing electronic filing		
E-Filing Tax Returns: Penalty Authority and Digitizing More Paper Return Data Could Increase Benefits (GAO-12-33)	http://www.gao.gov/products/GAO-12-33	IS, ISR, IFB
Electronic Tax Return Filing: Improvements Can Be Made before Mandate Becomes Fully Implemented (GAO-11-344)	http://www.gao.gov/products/GAO-11-344	IS, IFB
Tax Administration: Opportunities Exist for IRS to Enhance Taxpayer Service and Enforcement for the 2010 Filing Season (GAO-09-1026)	http://www.gao.gov/products/GAO-09-1026	ISR
Tax Administration: 2007 Filing Season Continues Trend of Improvement, but Opportunities to Reduce Costs and Increase Tax Compliance Should Be Evaluated (GAO-08-38)	http://www.gao.gov/products/GAO-08-38	ISR
Enhancing electronic filing and improving accuracy of paid preparers		
Tax Administration: Many Taxpayers Rely on Tax Software and IRS Needs to Assess Associated Risks (GAO-09-297)	http://www.gao.gov/products/GAO-09-297	IFB
Enhancing internal controls		
Management Report: Improvements Are Needed to Enhance the Internal Revenue Service's Internal Controls and Operating Effectiveness (GAO-11-494R)	http://www.gao.gov/products/GAO-11-494R	IS, IFB
Enhancing taxpayer services		
2011 Tax Filing: Processing Gains, but Taxpayer Assistance Could Be Enhanced by More Self-Service Tools (GAO-12-176)	http://www.gao.gov/products/GAO-12-176	ISR
Expanding use of math error authority or third party data		
2011 Tax Filing: IRS Dealt with Challenges to Date but Needs Additional Authority to Verify Compliance (GAO-11-481)	http://www.gao.gov/products/GAO-11-481	IR

Report title and number	Website for current status of matters and/or recommendations	Potential financial impact
Recovery Act: IRS Quickly Implemented Tax Provisions, but Reporting and Enforcement Improvements Are Needed (GAO-10-349)	http://www.gao.gov/products/GAO-10-349	ISR
Tax Administration: IRS's 2008 Filing Season Generally Successful Despite Challenges, although IRS Could Expand Enforcement during Returns Processing (GAO-09-146)	http://www.gao.gov/products/GAO-09-146	ISR
2009 Tax Filing Season: IRS Met Many 2009 Goals, but Telephone Access Remained Low, and Taxpayer Service and Enforcement Could Be Improved (GAO-10-225)	http://www.gao.gov/products/GAO-10-225	IR, ISR
Implementing Information Reporting and Document Matching (IRDM) system		
IRS Management: Cost Estimate for New Information Reporting System Needs to be Made More Reliable (GAO-12-59)	http://www.gao.gov/products/GAO-12-59	IFB
Information Reporting: IRS Could Improve Cost Basis and Transaction Settlement Reporting Implementation (GAO-11-557)	http://www.gao.gov/products/GAO-11-557	IFB
Implementing Patient Protection and Affordable Care Act (PPACA)		
Patient Protection and Affordable Care Act: IRS Should Expand Its Strategic Approach to Implementation (GAO-11-719)	http://www.gao.gov/products/GAO-11-719	IFB
Improving corporate tax compliance		
Tax Gap: Actions Needed to Address Noncompliance with S-Corporation Tax Rules (GAO-10-195)	http://www.gao.gov/products/GAO-10-195	IR, IFB
Improving individual or corporate tax compliance		
Financial Derivatives: Disparate Tax Treatment and Information Gaps Create Uncertainty and Potential Abuse (GAO-11-750)	http://www.gao.gov/products/GAO-11-750	IFB
Federal Tax Collection: Potential for Using Passport Issuance to Increase Collection of Unpaid Taxes (GAO-11-272)	http://www.gao.gov/products/GAO-11-272	IR
Improving international tax administration		
Tax Administration: IRS's Information Exchanges with Other Countries Could Be Improved through Better Performance Information (GAO-11-730)	http://www.gao.gov/products/GAO-11-730	IFB
Improving management of information technology (IT) investments		
Investment Management: IRS Has a Strong Oversight Process but Needs to Improve How It Continues Funding Ongoing Investments (GAO-11-587)	http://www.gao.gov/products/GAO-11-587	IS, IFB
Improving real estate tax compliance		
Tax Administration: Expanded Information Reporting Could Help IRS Address Compliance Challenges with Forgiven Mortgage Debt (GAO-10-997)	http://www.gao.gov/products/GAO-10-997	IR
Home Mortgage Interest Deduction: Despite Challenges Presented by Complex Tax Rules, IRS Could Enhance Enforcement and Guidance (GAO-09-769)	http://www.gao.gov/products/GAO-09-769	IR

Report title and number	Website for current status of matters and/or recommendations	Potential financial impact
Real Estate Tax Deduction: Taxpayers Face Challenges in Determining What Qualifies; Better Information Could Improve Compliance (GAO-09-521)	http://www.gao.gov/products/GAO-09-521	IR
Improving rental real estate compliance		
Tax Gap: Actions That Could Improve Rental Real Estate Reporting Compliance (GAO-08-956)	http://www.gao.gov/products/GAO-08-956	IR
Improving sole proprietors' compliance		
Tax Gap: Limiting Sole Proprietor Loss Deductions Could Improve Compliance but Would Also Limit Some Legitimate Losses (GAO-09-815)	http://www.gao.gov/products/GAO-09-815	IFB
Improving third party compliance		
Tax Gap: IRS Could Do More to Promote Compliance by Third Parties with Miscellaneous Income Reporting Requirements (GAO-09-238)	http://www.gao.gov/products/GAO-09-238	IR, IFB
Improving use of whistleblower claims		
Tax Whistleblowers: Incomplete Data Hinders IRS's Ability to Manage Claim Processing Time and Enhance External Communication (GAO-11-683)	http://www.gao.gov/products/GAO-11-683	IR, IFB
Increasing collection of unpaid payroll taxes		
Tax Compliance: Businesses Owe Billions in Federal Payroll Taxes (GAO-08-617)	http://www.gao.gov/products/GAO-08-617	IFB
Increasing tax debt collection		
Tax Debt Collection: IRS Needs to Better Manage the Collection Notices Sent to Individuals (GAO-09-976)	http://www.gao.gov/products/GAO-09-976	ISR
Promoting effective use of third-party data		
Tax Gap: IRS Has Modernized Its Business Nonfiler Program but Could Benefit from More Evaluation and Use of Third-Party Data (GAO-10-950)	http://www.gao.gov/products/GAO-10-950	IR, IFB
Reducing tax evasion		
Tax Gap: IRS Can Improve Efforts to Address Tax Evasion by Networks of Businesses and Related Entities (GAO-10-968)	http://www.gao.gov/products/GAO-10-968	IFB

Legend: IR – Increase revenue, IS – Increase savings, ISR – Increase savings and revenue, IFB – Indirect financial benefit.

Source: GAO.

Notes: Products with open matters and recommendations identified as of March 19, 2012. Some products may have matters and/or recommendations that do not have potential financial benefits or could be placed in different categories than provided above.

Appendix VII: GAO Contact and Staff Acknowledgments

GAO Contact	James R. White, (202) 512-9110 or WhiteJ@gao.gov
Staff Acknowledgments	In addition to the contact named above, Libby Mixon, Assistant Director; Mark Abraham; Amy Bowser; Dean Campbell; Mary Fike; Sairah Ijaz; Erik Kjeldgaard; Paul Middleton; Ed Nannenhorn; Sabine Paul; Cynthia Saunders; Mark Ryan; and Robyn Trotter made key contributions to this report.

Please Print on Recycled Paper.

www.ingramcontent.com/pod-product-compliance
Lightning Source LLC
Chambersburg PA
CBHW081137290526
45795CB00006B/2274